Contents

KU-200-766

About the author

Patricia McBride is a writer and independent training consultant, specialising in management and interpersonal skills training. She runs training courses for people applying for jobs and for managers who recruit staff.

Patricia is the author of a companion book to this one *Excel at Interviews* and is also the author of *The Emotional Intelligence Activities Pack* from Lifetime Publishing.

Acknowledgements

I would like to thank the following people for giving their time and assistance in writing this book:

Rick Leggatt, Debbie Gregory and Jim Machon.

Thanks also to Cambridgeshire County Council for allowing me to reproduce their application form.

CVs and Applications

Patricia McBride

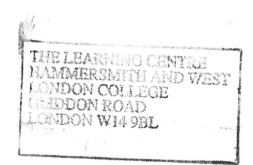
Student Helpbook Series

Lifetime
Publishing

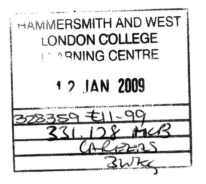
CVs and Applications – sixth edition

Published by Lifetime Publishing, Mill House, Stallard Street, Trowbridge BA14 8HH

© Nord Anglia Lifetime Development South West Ltd, 2007

ISBN 978-1904979203

Printed and bound by Cromwell Press Ltd, Trowbridge

Cover design by Jane Norman

Illustrations by Royston Robertson

Chapter one

Creative job-search ideas

You should read this chapter if you:

- can't find the job you want through advertisements or the 'normal' methods
- want to brush up your knowledge of traditional job-search methods
- want to widen your chances of finding exactly the right job.

By the end of this chapter you should know how:

- and where to find jobs through advertisements, agencies and the internet
- to use networking, face to face and on the web

- to write speculative ('on spec') letters to potential employers
- to use some innovative ideas to get noticed
- to use email appropriately
- to advertise yourself on the web.

Make your search successful

It is said that less than half the jobs available at any one time are advertised. This means that you must be willing to look wider than your newspaper to find just the job for you. In this chapter we explore where to find jobs through both traditional and other routes.

If you are seeking an Apprenticeship, many training providers now expect you to find your own employer.

Advertisements in newspapers

Naturally, your local paper is a good starting point if you want to work locally. Find out what night they advertise jobs, and also check out if any free newspapers carry advertisements. National papers also advertise jobs.

Science, engineering and technology	Marketing and sales
Guardian – Thursday *Telegraph* – Tuesday and Thursday	*Guardian* – Monday *Times* – Thursday *Independent* – Tuesday *Telegraph* – Thursday
Public sector *Guardian* – Wednesday *Times* – Tuesday *Telegraph* – Thursday and Sunday	**IT** *Guardian* – Thursday *Observer* – Sunday *Times* – Thursday *Independent* – Monday
Business and finance *Observer* – Sunday *Times* – Thursday *Independent* – Wednesday *Telegraph* – Thursday	**Creative and media** *Guardian* – Monday *Times* – Thursday *Independent* – Tuesday
Education and research *Guardian* – Tuesday *Times* – Tuesday and Thursday *Independent* – Thursday	**Jobs supplement** *Guardian* – Saturday *Observer* – Sunday *Times* – Thursday *Telegraph* – Thursday

Accounting	**Charities**
Telegraph – Monday	*Guardian* – Wednesday
Independent – Tuesday and Sunday	
Financial Times – Wednesday	
Times – Thursday and Sunday	
General graduate appointments	**Health**
Telegraph – Monday, Tuesday, Thursday and Sunday	*Guardian* – Wednesday
Independent – Thursday and Sunday	
Guardian – Saturday	
Times – Sunday	
Housing	**Legal**
Guardian – Wednesday	*Times* – Tuesday and Sunday
Times – Friday and Sunday	*Independent* – Wednesday
Secretarial	**Social services**
Times – Monday, Wednesday and Thursday	*Guardian* – Wednesday
Guardian – Monday and Saturday	

Professional journals

Do remember that many vacancies are advertised in professional journals. You can find many of these in your main library. Alternatively, contact the journal and ask how you can subscribe or if they have a web page showing appointments.

Your college or workers who already work in the field should be able to tell you the names of suitable journals. If you can't find one, you could look in a writers' book called *The Writers' and Artists' Yearbook* – you'll find one in your main library. They list details of the bigger journals.

Connexions and Jobcentre Plus

Connexions have jobs for 16- to 19-year-olds: look on the web or in your phone book for their contact details.

If you are older, try Jobcentre Plus: again you can find contact details online or in your phone book.

Employment agencies

There are many, many employment agencies that between them hold thousands of jobs that are not advertised. Some agencies are generalists – they hold different types of vacancy, whilst others specialise only in jobs in one particular field. To find where the agencies are for local jobs look in your *Yellow Pages* or similar directory. For work further afield look in professional journals or on the internet for details of relevant agencies.

Jobs on the web

Many organisations now advertise their vacancies on the web. Surfing round the web you will find sites from:

- employment agencies
- universities
- organisations seeking to fill their own vacancies. Organisations are increasingly only advertising on the web as it saves the very high cost of advertising in newspapers
- professional bodies.

The web has very many sites for looking for jobs. If you don't know any suitable sites I suggest you start by going to www.google.com or www.google.co.uk or your favourite search engine. If you want to search by locality, type in something like 'Jobs Cambridge' (remember to click on 'pages from the UK'). If you want to search by type of job, type something like 'Jobs Engineering'. If you are not sure what type of job you want, type in 'Jobs UK' and sites covering a wide variety of jobs will appear in the search engine list.

Jobs for people with disabilities

If you have a disability, you can also look for jobs online. Searching for a few minutes in Google I found www.disabledworkers.org.uk/alezaportal1/default2.asp?tree=2044, which listed jobs for disabled people sector by sector. Remember that your local Jobcentre Plus should be able to offer you help and guidance.

Useful organisations for jobseekers with disabilities

This is just a selection of the many organisations that will be able to help you.

- Disability Action – www.disabilityaction.org (offers information and support for people with disabilities)
- Employers Forum on Disability – www.employers-forum.co.uk
- Directgov – www.direct.gov.org
- Employment Opportunities – www.opportunities.org.uk

You will find many more sites by simply typing 'employment opportunities disabled' into your favourite search engine.

Networking – what it is, how to do it

One way to find out about unadvertised jobs is called 'networking'. Networking is simply using (in the nicest possible sense) people you know, and people they know, to discover what opportunities are available.

Even better, these people may be able to recommend you to the shortlister, and so help you bypass many other people who are also looking for jobs. Your objective is to get to meet the people who are the decision-makers about filling posts.

Whenever you speak to people, consider them as possible sources of information about job opportunities. This is true whether you are speaking to friends, family, family friends, other students, tutors, neighbours or whoever. Many of them will be in paid employment. They will know, or can find out, what job openings there may be in their organisations.

Alternatively, they may be friends with people who are knowledgeable about other companies, and this can be just as useful.

Some people find speaking about job opportunities to others they know embarrassing. But remember that the 'old-boys' network' has been making life smooth for the people in it for centuries. Furthermore, many employers appreciate knowing someone who can fill a post. It saves them the trouble and expense of advertising.

Networking – getting started

Write yourself a plan of action. Begin with ten possible contacts. These can be people you know or know of. (Some of your contacts may be through the web – more about that later in this chapter.) Ask yourself these questions: 'How will I get in touch with these people?', 'What will I say?'. Remember, these people may not be in a position to offer you a job themselves, but they should be able to give you other contacts and tips on how best to approach them. They may also be able to put in a word for you, give you up-to-date job market information, and suggest ideas you've overlooked or ways to improve your presentation skills. Ask them if you can use their name when making an approach, as that can be a good way to introduce yourself.

A good idea is to set yourself a goal that each of these ten people will put you in touch with at least two other people. Continue like this and you will see that you can quickly make contact with a huge number of people. Some contacts will be easy – you'll actually meet the person through your everyday life. Start with the friendliest person – this will give you more confidence to go on to other more difficult contacts.

Recording networking

With a number of such conversations, you'll start gaining quite a lot of information, so it's important to be organised. Use a card index system or file on your computer (anything that works for you) to keep details of the contacts and what you find out. Here is the information you will need to note:

Name:	Job title:
Organisation:	How contact was made:
Contact details:	
Possible vacancies:	Contact date:
Additional information:	Follow-up action:

Update this information every time you contact someone. And file the information in alphabetical order under the name of the organisation so you can easily find it again.

Sound positive

Each time you speak to a contact – even if it's not actually the person who may be able to offer you the job – sound positive and professional.

Be prepared at all times to talk about your skills and strengths – you never know what information may be passed on to the decision-maker.

Telephone contacts

Before you pick up the phone, rehearse what you are going to say. If you are likely to get nervous, jot down the key points on a piece of paper to prompt you. Here are some tips for using the telephone.

- Choose a phone in a quiet location.
- If using a payphone, have plenty of change available or use a phone-card.

- If using a mobile, make sure it is topped up and don't walk along as you make the call.

- Sit or stand up straight and smile as you say hello (your posture and facial expressions alter the way your voice sounds – you can hear a smile).

- Address the person by name.

- Explain the reason for your call.

- Mention the name of your contact.

- Ask if it's a good time to call – offer to call another time if necessary.

- Have your discussion (see below for typical questions to ask).

- Be polite and professional at all times.

- Try to arrange a meeting to get further information and advice.

- If you can't arrange a meeting and they can't help at this time ask their permission to call back at a later date to ask again.

- Thank the person for their time.

- Write down the results of your contact on your index card.

If you feel worried about doing this, practise with a friend first.

Questions to ask

If you are successful and your contact gives you some time to discuss a potential vacancy (even if none exists at present), have a few questions in mind. These might include the following.

- What does the job involve?

- What type of person are you looking for?

- Who would be the line manager or supervisor?

- What is a typical working day/week like?

- What induction training is available?

- What continuing training is offered?

- What career paths would be possible?

- What are the current and future issues for that organisation/ business sector?

- What type of qualifications would help me to get a job in that organisation?
- What particular skills are you looking for?
- What is the best way to obtain these skills without currently being employed by the organisation?
- How can I be informed of vacancies as soon as they occur?

Following through

When you make a contact, always send a polite letter thanking the person for their time and telling them if you have followed up any advice or contacts they gave you. This need only be a short letter but it is common courtesy and another way of being remembered, which may be important in future. Attach a copy of your CV.

Asking for a meeting

There will come a time when you get to speak to the decision-maker. He or she may be the personnel manager or head of department. Whether on the phone, or speaking face to face, you will have to judge whether or not it is appropriate to have a lengthy discussion about any vacancies. If the person is willing but doesn't have time at that moment, try to arrange a time to meet or phone when they're less busy. Consider the phone conversation below – you sense that the person you're calling is busy, so this is how you tackle it:

You

'Hello Mr Patel. My name is Amy Thomas. Dorothy Edwards suggested I contact you for a chat about job possibilities. Is this a good time to talk or can I arrange to call back another time?'

Mr Patel

'Dorothy told me you might call. I can spare you a few minutes.'

You

'Thanks very much. I know that you're not advertising for a customer service clerk at the moment, but this is the type of work I'm really interested in and I wondered if there were likely to be any vacancies.'

Mr Patel

'Not as far as I know.'

You

'Well, one reason I'm phoning you in particular is because I know quite a bit about your company from Mrs Edwards and of course from your products. Even though you don't have any vacancies just now, would it be possible for me to take up 20 minutes of your time one day to discuss how I can be in the best position for getting a job with you when one comes up?'

Mr Patel

'Well, I'm really busy, but ... well, okay. What about the 14th at 3.30pm? I'll pencil you in for 15 minutes.'

You

'Thank you so much. I'll look forward to meeting you then.'

The trick here was to persevere without sounding pushy. But however well rehearsed you are, the answer can sometimes be a clear 'no'. In this case, thank the person politely and ask if you could contact them again in a few weeks' time if you're still looking for a job. Also ask if they could suggest someone else you could speak to in your search for a job. If you succeed in arranging a meeting, then well done! Prepare for it well. Although this is not a job interview it is important to take the meeting seriously. Plan ahead what you are going to say and what you want to get from the meeting. Dress smartly and arrive punctually. Give the contact person an overview of yourself, your career history (if any) and your skills. What you say may begin something like this:

You

'Thank you for seeing me, Ms Holmes. I know that you don't have any clerical vacancies at the moment but as you know I'd be very interested in applying when one comes up. If I tell you a bit about myself you may be able to give me some advice about any other skills or qualifications I might need.

I've just completed a City and Guilds in business administration. I got good marks for all my coursework and my placement with Jones Insurance went very well. In fact Mrs Dawes there gave me a reference and I've brought a copy along for you. I feel pretty confident I have a good grasp of the skills you need and I'm a very enthusiastic and hard worker. I learn fast too ...'

When you feel you've said enough, you may be asked some further questions about yourself. In turn, ask about the company a bit more, what kind of people they look for as employees, and advice on what additional experience you should gain to get you the job you want. Ask if they can suggest anyone else you can contact in your job search. Do remember to thank the person for their time and follow up the meeting with a polite thank-you letter. Remember to record your meeting in your information file for future reference.

Networking on the web

Web networking has much in common with other networking. One big disadvantage though is that you won't be able to impress people with your charm or the power of your voice. It's important therefore to make the web work best for you. Here are a few tips:

- write grammatically

- keep your writing focused – be clear about what you want from the other person (and what you can offer in return if there is anything)

- act respectfully towards others at all times, value the time and effort they have put into communicating with you

- give yourself time to build up your network, don't leave it until your studies are almost over or you're out of a job.

Like any networking, work from a position of strength. That works best when you are currently employed or still a student. If you are unemployed, try to undertake temporary or voluntary work so that you look more appealing to those you contact. It doesn't matter if the work is part-time – the other person won't know that.

Where to network online

The most obvious answer is with people whose email address you know. Keep in touch with people who may be in a position to help, and think about what you may be able to offer them in return. Ask your email contacts if they can suggest anyone else you can contact.

There are thousands of discussion groups so you'll be sure to find one in your interest area – and if you can't you can always start one ...

Through discussion groups you can be in touch with literally dozens of people in no time. You may even get in touch with people who work for your target companies. Remember that your conversations will be public, so be polite, professional and confident at all times.

Networking by email

Sometimes your networking contacts give you email addresses rather than telephone numbers. If you contact people by email, it is essential that you carefully plan what you are going to write. You can use the questions in the 'Questions to ask' section on page 11 earlier in this chapter to help you to plan what to say. You should also read the section on 'Writing 'on spec" on page 16 of this chapter, as this contains many useful ideas. Remember, even if your approach is a general query, you should attach or include your CV, which should be professionally presented. See Chapter four for more details of how to write CVs.

USENET

USENET is a compilation of newsgroups resembling electronic bulletin-board systems. Businesses list job openings on a relevant newsgroup, although currently many of the vacancies are in the computer field.

Email etiquette – top tips

It can be tempting to be very informal when sending an email to a prospective employer, because most of our emails are to friends and people we know well. However, a prospective employer will not know you and you must take as much care as if you were writing a traditional letter.

- Make sure you use the correct email address. Try to find out the address of the person who is responsible for the vacancy, but if that fails use the general email for the organisation. BUT it's a good idea not to fill this in until your email is complete. You don't want to accidentally hit the 'send' button when your email is only partly completed. It makes you look bad.

- State the job title in the subject bar, along with any reference.

- Use the person's title – *Mr, Mrs, Dr* or whatever. If you don't know who you are addressing it to, send it to *Sir* or *Madam*. If you don't know their title, assume a man is *Mr* and a woman is *Ms*.

- Be concise. Plan your approach and get your main selling points across quickly and effectively.

- Lay out the email as if it were a letter.

- Be professional. Don't use abbreviations unless you are sure the person will know them. NEVER use text spelling. Check all spelling, punctuation, etc. Don't use emoticons ('smileys'). Make sure your tone is polite and friendly, but not too informal.

- Don't write in CAPITALS – some people see it as shouting, and don't use underlining – it makes it more difficult to read.

- Consider pasting any attachments into the **body** of your email, as many people won't open an attachment because of viruses.

- Consider whether your email address is professional. If it is cutesy or suggestive, you may want to use another one.

- Check your email very carefully before you send it off.

Safety

Remember safety guidelines at all times when communicating with someone on the web. Do not arrange to meet anyone without first telling a parent or an adult you know and trust.

You might also like to look on www.jobsearch.about.com/mpchat.html

Writing 'on spec'

An often overlooked way to find a job is simply to write to an organisation and ask if they've got one. This is known as writing speculatively, more commonly known as 'on spec'. If you don't know of any vacancies at the moment, this can be very worthwhile. Many organisations keep such letters (which should be sent to them with a copy of your CV) on file. This saves them advertising when a vacancy occurs; they simply contact all the people who have sent in details. But be warned, under the Data Protection Act they have to destroy such letters after six months unless you give them specific permission to keep them. This means that you should make a note to send them an updated version every six months.

Take this example. If you want to get into hotel management, you could write to all the big hotel chains – and indeed your local hotels – asking what openings they have. You have nothing to lose but a little time and a few stamps. You might gain a lot.

If you are writing 'on spec', be clear about what sort of job you seek, or say if you are willing to consider anything they might have to offer. If you are looking for a particular type of work, write the letter very much with that in mind and enclose a CV that is adapted for the type of work you seek. Be polite, but don't be overly humble or the reader may not believe you have the confidence and experience to do the job.

As you will see later in this chapter, it is useful to follow up on speculative letters with a phone call. In practical terms, this means that you shouldn't send off more letters than you can follow up. If you realistically couldn't make more than, say, 15 phone calls a week, then limit your letters to that number if you really want to maximise your chances.

'I needed to earn some money while studying, and unemployment was high at that time. I wrote to 12 restaurants where I live, sending my CV. Over the next three months, eight of them contacted me.'

Quote from a student at a further education college

Targeted 'on spec' letters

An alternative way to write 'on spec' letters is to target them to a particular organisation as a response to something you know about the company. This could be an article you have seen in a newspaper or trade or professional magazine, or something you have learned about by word of mouth.

Here are a few beginnings of targeted 'on spec' letters:

Dear Mr Thomas

I read with interest in this week's Daily Telegraph that your company has just won a big contract to supply Hokomoto with parts for their engines. It occurs to me that in the light of your increased workload you may be looking for more administrative staff. I am...

or

Dear Ms Cohen

This week's Hotels Monthly mentions that you are planning to open a hotel in my area within the next three months. I have recently finished...

or

Dear Mr Briggs

This week's Bloxford Recorder mentioned that your company is planning to expand into other areas of the fashion industry. I am...

Sample 'on spec' letter

James Prior
33 Church Street
Oldham
OL3 4RR

Mrs S Smith
Big Inn
23-45 High Street
Oldham
OL4 4RE

(today's date)

Dear Mrs Smith

Secretarial/clerical vacancies

I am writing to ask if you have any secretarial or clerical vacancies at the moment. As you will see from my enclosed CV, I am just about to leave Blackdown College and have completed an NVQ level 2 in administration.

This has given me some very relevant skills including:
– typing at 40 wpm
– knowledge of general office procedures
– ability to use Word, Excel and PowerPoint.

I did a work placement at Dublin Manufacturers, and Mr Bower, the office manager, has given me a reference, which I enclose. As you will see, he found me enthusiastic, quick to learn and flexible.

Working for your company particularly interests me because it has an excellent reputation for being ahead of the field, and I feel sure that I could make a positive contribution to your work.

If you have no vacancies at present, I should be very grateful if you would keep my details on file and let me know when one occurs.

Yours sincerely

James Prior

By responding to changes in the circumstances of an organisation, you will be showing that you have your ear to the ground, and have read the right newspapers and journals. This shows considerable initiative and would impress most potential employers.

Follow-up calls

Whichever type of 'on spec' letter you send, do follow it up with a phone call a few days later. Have your letter at hand and ask to speak to the person to whom you wrote. Introduce yourself, explain why you're ringing, and find out whether it is a convenient time to talk. Your aim is to get the person's response to your letter. If it is positive, ask if you can meet to discuss it further, or whether you should complete an application form. If it isn't, then all is not lost. You can ask for your details to be kept on file.

If the person hasn't had time to read the letter, ask when it would be convenient to call back. Thank them for their time, and if you are using networking techniques described earlier in this chapter, record your call in your card index or other system.

Blowing all the rules

If you seek work in a creative field and are exceptionally original, consider breaking all the rules in this book! Maybe you can write a covering letter that will make you stand out by its sheer originality and creativity. Try to link it to the type of work you want to do.

- Want to work in publishing?

  Design yourself a book cover with your details on the back! (Think of an original and meaningful title for the book Job-Search Techniques by (your name), Seeking Success by (your name) and so on.)

- Want to work in advertising?

  Write an advertisement for yourself.

- Want to work in graphic design?

  Design a poster telling about yourself.

- Want to work in fabric design?

  Send a sample of fabric you've made, perhaps incorporating your name.

- Want to work in computing?

  Design a web page for yourself and send a copy of the home page and the URL.

You might even like to consider going really crazy and drawing a cartoon CV. Whilst this sort of CV may not be conventional, many employers would be curious about someone who could so cleverly tell you so much about themselves. I saw a really excellent cartoon CV, and the author always got offered an interview.

For more details of writing a covering letter to include with your CV see Chapter nine.

The web as a marketing tool

Web marketing is not for novices, as designing a web page can be tricky. However, it is a growing trend and is of obvious benefit if you are in the IT world. It would be unwise to rely solely on this method of job search unless you are in an industry where this is the norm. See it as an additional tool to use alongside traditional methods if it is right for you.

When you are applying for jobs remember to send your web address and also consider sending some pages with your CV or application form, if appropriate. You could certainly take them with you to the interview.

It follows that you must take as much care with your web page design as you would with any other job-search method. A poor web page is unlikely to get any prospective employer picking up the phone or emailing you in response. For that reason, only attempt a page if you are sure you can do a good job or get someone else to design one for you.

Advantages of a web page

Increasingly common, web-page self marketing is a real bonus. Many employers are competent on the internet and you can include details of your web page in any information you send them. They'll be impressed!

Other advantages are that you can show samples of your work on your web pages – this is your web portfolio. The site itself will also demonstrate your skills, and you can show that you are very up to date.

Some DOs and DON'Ts

Do make sure that:

- your web page is up and running before you give the address to prospective employers

- everything on your website is professional, from your CV to the graphics

- your site works – all links do just that

- your website is coherent – it sticks to one theme so that prospective employers are clear what you're offering

- you make separate links for each section of your web page – remember to put all these links on your opening page; links might include your CV, testimonials, references and samples of your work

- you use both graphics and text

- you follow safe guidelines on web, see www.thinkuknow.co.uk/ for advice.

Don't:

- include a copy of your photograph – employers could be open to charges of discrimination

- include irrelevant information.

What to include

There are no hard and fast rules about web design for job search. This means that you have a free hand to show your creativity. And if you're not sure what to include, look for examples already existing on the web for inspiration.

Buying web-building expertise

Maybe you've decided to pay someone to design a web page for you. To find someone reliable, you could start in no better place than on the web. Look for designers whose work you like. If you can't tell who designed a web page, the information may be 'hidden' at the top of the home page. Most browsers have a 'View Source' or 'View HTML' option and it may reveal the designer's name.

Alternatively, ask around: a personal reference is often best. Make sure you get a quote before you start and that you're happy that the designer can meet your deadline. Another tip – remember that your web page may need updating regularly. If this is true for you, don't ask a college friend who may vanish when the course ends.

Chapter checklist

To search for jobs creatively you should:

- look at advertisements in newspaper, journals and magazines

- ask employers if you can see their internal job advertising list

- contact employment agencies

- contact your Jobcentre Plus or Connexions service

- network – use contacts to find out details of people who may be able to help you with your job search, these contacts can be personal or via the internet

- use vacancies chatrooms, web forums and mailing lists to increase your chances of networking effectively – remember when using chatlines to follow safety advice and don't arrange to meet anyone without warning your parents or an adult you know and trust

- use your contacts both for details of jobs and advice on how best to present yourself

- always prepare yourself in advance for either a face-to-face or telephone conversation with a contact

- follow up a contact with a thank-you letter

- ask your contact if they know of any other possible contacts, if they can't help you themselves

- have a system for recording your contacts

- write 'on spec' to organisations you'd like to work for, enclosing your CV

- write to organisations in the news (unless it's for redundancies!) – they may be taking on more staff

- be positive, remembering that you are worth employing

- take notice of email etiquette

- think of creative ways to get yourself noticed

- consider using a web page to market yourself.

Chapter two

Analysing yourself and your STAR competencies

You should read this chapter:

- before you begin to complete an application form or write a CV.

By the end of this chapter you should know:

- how to analyse your skills, experience, personality, likes and dislikes

- where to turn to for help with this analysis

- how to identify key (STAR) activities to demonstrate your competencies

- how to present your successes effectively
- how to deal with difficult information about yourself
- how to sell your leisure activities
- how to use words in a winning way.

Your goal

No employer would take on a new member of staff without interviewing them first. Many universities interview prospective students too, rather than selecting them purely on the basis of their grades and application forms. When you present yourself on paper, in the form of a CV or an application form, what you are trying to do is to sell yourself. This means that, generally speaking, your goal in presenting yourself on paper is to get an interview. All the information in this chapter is equally valuable for university, job or Apprenticeship applications, as well as for compiling a CV.

Self analysis

So, let's have a good look at this product you have to sell – you! Imagine for a moment a person who has to interview candidates for a job or university place. He or she is looking to 'buy' (or select for interview) the best possible person. Unless they happen to know any candidate, each person at this stage is simply a collection of facts. Initially, the shortlister will be looking for some basic requirements. These are: (a) what you can offer, (b) your strengths, (c) your weak points and (d) your attributes and how they match the job they have to offer.

'Sometimes I get so frustrated because I know that the candidates must have the skills I need from the jobs they have done, but because they haven't told me I can't shortlist them.'

Quote from a local authority manager

My skills

Let's start your self-analysis on a positive note – focusing on what you can do. Once you've read the lists of skills-related words or statements that follow, it's a good idea for you to make notes of those that apply to you. In fact it is useful to keep a special notebook to record your thoughts and ideas about your skills and competencies. You will find further suggestions to write in your notebook as you work through this book. (You could keep your notebook with your record of achievement materials.)

In your notebook, write a list of everything you can do. Things you can do are your *skills;* you don't have to be perfect at them, just reasonably competent. What follows are categories of skills as a prompt – you will probably be able to add to them. To help you to remember all your skills (you may not have used all of them recently or consciously thought about them as skills), make a list of as many different tasks you have completed as possible. For example, have you undertaken any project at school or college that required skills not usually used? What skills have you used for studying or in jobs you have done? What skills have you developed just from being with people, or from helping around the house, or with children?

Communication skills

- listening well
- communicating clearly
- teaching others
- speaking clearly
- speaking in groups
- calming others
- writing legibly
- explaining complicated ideas
- translating
- writing analytically
- defending yourself
- having clear, easy-to-read handwriting
- writing concisely
- putting across an opposing viewpoint
- proofreading accurately

Activity

Identify two communication skills you already possess. If you are not sure ask others to help you.

Practical skills

- fixing cars
- filing
- keyboarding
- driving
- carpentry
- first aid
- cooking
- riding a bike
- laying bricks
- plastering
- sewing
- swimming
- using a computer
- painting
- metalwork
- demonstrating
- knitting

Activity

Identify two practical skills you already possess.

Financial skills

- budgeting
- paying bills
- calculating
- evaluating

- understanding the banking system
- analysing

Activity

Identify two financial skills you already possess.

People skills

- caring for the disadvantaged
- cooperating with people
- challenging
- being empathetic
- leading
- advising
- organising
- team-building
- supporting others
- motivating
- liaising
- mentoring
- counselling

Activity

Identify two people skills you already possess.

Creative skills

- drawing
- painting
- producing
- designing
- singing
- dancing
- decorating

- composing
- inventing
- choreographing
- photography
- acting
- modelling
- playing an instrument
- developing
- writing creatively
- document layout
- web designing

Activity

Identify two creative skills you already possess.

Thinking skills

- editing
- originating
- analysing
- conceiving
- planning
- imagining
- programming
- investigating
- sorting
- researching
- devising
- enquiring
- designing

- questioning
- preparing
- examining
- scheming
- exploring
- shaping
- inspecting
- formulating

Activity

Identify two thinking skills you already possess.

Activity – SWOT

Spend a few minutes undertaking a SWOT analysis of your skills. SWOT is a mnemonic for **S**trengths, **W**eaknesses, **O**pportunities and **T**hreats. This type of analysis can be useful for all sorts of decision making. Copy the grid below into your notebook and complete each section.

Strengths (what I'm good at)	**Weaknesses** (skills I'd like to be better at)
Opportunities (to use my strengths and overcome my weaknesses)	**Threats** (to using my strengths and overcoming my weaknesses)

My personal qualities

Employers increasingly realise that your personal qualities are of crucial importance. For example, employing someone who has good technical skills, but who sulks, bullies others, is lazy, etc, will not be good for business and will demotivate their colleagues. Here is a list of typical qualities employers are looking for:

- ability to work as part of a team
- ability to use initiative
- cheerful
- 'can do' approach
- proactive in looking for work to do
- good at problem solving
- willing to ask for help when necessary
- friendly
- mature in attitude
- energetic
- good communicator
- willing to learn
- tenacious
- reliable
- sympathetic
- consistent
- helpful
- careful
- open-minded
- comfortable with change
- perceptive
- self-controlled
- optimistic
- self-aware
- self-motivated

'I'd rather take on someone with a slightly lower level of skills and a good personality, than a technically brilliant person who would be a nightmare to work with. It's easier to teach technical skills than how to be a decent person.'

Quote from a human resources manager

Activity

Look at the list of personal qualities above and score yourself out of ten for each item. Congratulate yourself on those items where you score highly. Now look at those items where your score is low. What steps can you take to improve your skills in these areas? Ask people who know you to help you if you are not sure.

My personality and competencies (behaviours)

Once you have listed your skills, you need to consider positive aspects of your personality. A large percentage of UK employers now use *competencies* to help them select staff. These competencies demonstrate the *behaviour* the candidate will show when undertaking work efficiently. For this reason competencies are sometimes called *behaviours*.

Below is a model that many people find useful when thinking about competencies:

- natural competencies – those to do with your characteristics and personality traits
- acquired competencies – those you have learned through education or experience
- adapting competencies – how you have applied your knowledge and skills throughout your career.

Many organisations will send you a list of the competencies they seek along with other information, such as the job description and person specification. They may well give you instructions as to which if these *selection criteria* you should address in your CV or application form.

STAR approach to competencies

STAR relates to incidents at work and stands for:

- **S**ituation – When, where, and with whom did the incident happen?

- **T**ask – Describe the task

- **A**ction – What action did YOU take to resolve the situation? (Remember to write about 'I', not 'we'.)

- **R**esult – What was the result of the action you took? What did you learn from the experience for the future?

Here are two examples:

Situation	When I worked for Hombell's Insurance company last summer...
Task	I was asked to sort out the filing system, which was totally disorganised.
Action	I asked people in the office what they thought the best way of filing the paperwork would be. I then recommended a method to the manager and explained what would be needed in the way of resources.
Result	She approved of this method. I began work two days later and completed the task within two weeks. It is estimated that the new system saves each worker approximately 15 minutes a day.

Example two (this one shows initiative):

Situation	My keyboarding skills were below what I felt was needed for the job.
Task	So I decided to improve them.
Action	I found an online course and practised for half of my lunch hour each day and whenever there was a quiet period.
Result	My typing speed is now 45 wpm, and I can now use many advanced features of Word, such as Tables, Mail Merge and Columns.

Using a STAR approach to presenting your information is particularly important when completing an application form. You should use it under the section headed something like 'Give information in support of your application' (see Chapter seven for more information). On a CV, you may only have enough space to simply list them. However, if any of your competencies are outstanding and particularly relevant you could include them in a section entitled 'Additional information' or 'Competencies'.

Activity

Identify your STAR stories for each of the following competencies:

Competency	Example
initiative	
team working	
dealing with conflict	
being creative	
taking the lead	
learning from difficulties	

My experience to date

Your list of 'experience' should to some extent overlap with your list of skills. If you are thinking 'what experience?' remember all the different things you have done. What jobs have you had? Have you:

- done any voluntary work, even informally?
- undertaken work shadowing?
- had special responsibility at school?
- had special responsibilities at home?
- travelled?
- had responsibilities as a member of a club?
- done something unusual?

Transferable skills and competencies

All of these experiences will have provided you with something relevant to offer an employer or university, if only something to talk about at interview. These are your *transferable skills and competencies*. That is, skills that you can *transfer* from one area of your life to another.

Let's look at two quite different examples. For the first, let's assume that you had two weeks' work experience as a receptionist in a hotel. Most receptionist jobs involve attending to guests, checking guests in and out, answering the phone and making bookings.

Receptionists may also undertake other office work, e.g. keyboarding. If we break down these examples we see that each has required more skills than was immediately obvious.

Attending to guests requires you to:

- have good communication skills
- work with members of the public
- be courteous
- be patient
- be able to respond to queries, perhaps at short notice
- deal with problems
- be able to cope with crises (double booking, people getting ill, etc)
- keep calm.

Checking residents in and out requires you to:

- be methodical
- write legibly, or make entries into the computer correctly
- communicate clearly
- respond to queries
- handle cash, credit cards, etc.

Answering the phone requires you to:

- have a good telephone manner
- take accurate messages
- respond effectively to the caller
- put calls through to the correct extension
- be efficient.

By looking at your experience in this way, you may also discover some skills you hadn't thought of before. Remember, a skill is simply something you can do. For example, it is a real skill to handle crisis situations effectively, and not everyone can be pleasant with awkward customers for eight hours at a stretch.

A second example might be newspaper delivery. On one level it seems a fairly humble occupation: after all, quite young adults take on this job. However, let's analyse the skills and personal qualities involved. Newspaper delivery involves:

- being prompt and reliable
- being able to work unsupervised
- being efficient – delivering the right paper to the right house
- being honest
- being polite to customers.

My likes and dislikes

You probably have enough experience of the world of work to know a bit about what you like and dislike. Think about any jobs, work experience or voluntary work (even unofficial) you have done. What did you enjoy? What excited you? What left you feeling bored? What did you positively hate? This type of analysis will not only help you to select a job, but also to sell yourself enthusiastically about those topics you enjoy.

Getting help with your analysis

Undertaking an analysis of your positive points can be a difficult task. For this reason you may like to think about getting help from others. Obviously, you need to ask people you can trust and who will give you an honest answer. Also, it makes sense to ask more than one person. Choose people who see you in different circumstances – a friend you socialise with would not see you in the same way as a teacher or employer, for example. Don't take everything people say at face value – really think about their comments. Do you agree with them? What examples could you give to back up the qualities or skills they have highlighted?

Using your Progress File

Some students have a Progress File (or similar file showing their record of achievement), which documents their academic and personal progress throughout their school career. If you have such a file, you should find plenty of things to use when writing CVs or completing application forms. You may be able to use it to think about your skills and personal development throughout the years – particularly in areas relevant to the job or course you are applying for.

Selling your leisure interests

So, how does identifying and recording your leisure interests help you with the application process? To answer this, let's look at university and job applications separately for a minute, then we'll look at ways in which you can write this section most effectively.

'I like to look at the leisure interests information candidates provide. It often gives me something to talk to them about at the beginning of the interview when I'm trying to get them to relax.'

Quote from a manager of a large retail company

University applications

The UCAS application does not specifically ask about leisure interests, although these could be included in the 'Personal statement' section. Chapter eight gives you advice on how to complete this.

Job applications and CVs

Most application forms have a section headed 'Leisure interests' or something similar. If, however, there is no such heading and you particularly want to tell the organisation about a leisure interest that is relevant to the job, you can always mention this in the covering letter you send with your form (see Chapter nine). Likewise, most people include a section in their CVs headed 'Leisure interests' or 'Additional information'.

Presenting leisure interests

For many people, finding something to say under this section is really difficult. You think to yourself, 'Well, all I do is watch television and go out with my mates!' Remember all the times when your teachers and parents said to you, 'You really should join something instead of sitting around every evening'? They weren't wrong ...

Still, let's see what we can make of your leisure activities that will look interesting to the shortlister.

Here are some common examples first:

'Watching television and going out with my friends.'

What does it say about you? Answer these questions:

- What types of television programmes do you like? – sport, national history, thrillers, films, soaps, game shows?

- What do you do when you go out with your friends? – drink, go to the cinema, go clubbing, attend sporting events, play sports, go to concerts?

Do any of your answers to the above relate in any way to the job or course you are interested in? If so, how?

Once you've thought through these questions your answer might now read:

'I enjoy watching television, especially detective stories and sport. I also enjoy seeing films. I socialise regularly with friends, often attending concerts or going bowling.'

This tells the shortlister that you follow some solitary pursuits (watching television), have several different interests (sports, detective stories, music) and you enjoy being with other people.

Here is another example:

'For the past six months I've been hitching around Europe with friends.'

This tells the prospective interviewer that you have initiative and drive; can find your way around; are independent; are flexible; (unless you had the whole trip planned in rigid detail before leaving) and can budget (unless, of course, you frequently wrote home for more funds!). Get the idea? Looked at this way, what may have seemed a good laugh and of no significance to your future career or education actually tells people quite a lot about you.

So, you could reword this statement as:

'I enjoy travelling and recently spent six months working my way around Europe with three friends. I particularly enjoy meeting people from other cultures, and the sense of challenge and change from day to day.'

'The work here involves people in fine detail work with their hands. I like to see if any of their hobbies require manual dexterity.'

Quote from a laboratory manager

Notice that these examples start with the word 'I'. The 'Leisure interests' section provides an opportunity for you to sell yourself as a real person, rather than a list of skills and qualifications. This is more effectively done by writing your interests as part of a personalised sentence, rather than simply listing 'reading, swimming, socialising, etc.'

Here are some other examples:

'I enjoy reading crime novels and watching science fictions films. I also like socialising with friends, often going to classical concerts or to cricket matches.'

'I am a keen sportswoman and belong to the school badminton team. I also play tennis and squash. I enjoy reading biographies and watching comedy films.'

'I enjoy model-making and belong to the local Model-Making Society. I like playing snooker and spending time with friends.'

'I very much like writing and belong to our local writers' group. I also enjoy reading, particularly political novels and crime stories.'

When you think about completing this section, ask yourself what the person reading it will be looking for. Some possible answers are:

- a sense that you are a 'rounded' person. This means that you have both solitary and social activities and a reasonably wide range of interests. This, it is hoped, indicates that you are able to work alone and/or with others.

- something to talk to you about in the interview. This is especially important for university interviews, when many applicants are saying similar things on their forms. The fact that you did something unusual will give the lecturer something to talk to you about.

- that your leisure interests in some way reflect the course or job you are applying for. This may be with a particular skill (for example, a practical hobby when applying for a practical job). Some employers actually say that this is the only thing they look for under this section. As you will not know in advance which approach to take you should put any directly relevant interests first in your list. If you put the others first, the reader might stop reading before they get to the good bits. Alternatively, it may be that the employer is looking for a personality trait that would be useful in the job (playing football may show that you work well as part of a team, for example).

Leisure interests – a word of caution

If you have interests that are likely to ring alarm bells with an employer, don't mention them. Such interests might include active membership of a political party, belonging to pressure groups, or a lot of involvement in dangerous sports (you might be off sick a lot with broken bones!).

'We know that some employers look at leisure interests and some don't, but it's impossible to anticipate who will and who won't. For that reason, it's important to make a good job of this section on every application form or CV.'

Careers teacher at a sixth form college

Activity

Now that you've read this section, make a list in your notebook of all your leisure interests, and spend some time working out the best way to present this information. Remember, your overall aim is to get an interview for that course or job.

By the way, don't worry if the leisure interest that springs to mind is not something you do regularly. As long as you have done/do it often enough to be able to talk about it sensibly at the interview, you should be okay.

Winning ways with words

By now, you should have a fair idea of the type of information you should present on paper, although there are more tips in later chapters. But for now, let's look at how to present this material effectively.

You've already had some help here (look back to the beginning of this chapter where there were lists of words to describe different skills and qualities). Thinking of your qualities and skills, work through these lists until you are happy that you have expressed yourself as accurately as possible.

Now look at the way you've wrapped up those words. Is the overall picture positive and lively or a bit bland? Look at these two examples:

'Reading, going to the cinema, socialising.'

Do you feel you know much about this person? Do they even enjoy these activities? Does her/his personality spring from the page? Compare this with:

I enjoy reading, particularly thrillers and science fiction. I also like socialising with friends, going to the cinema and concerts.'

Still fairly brief, but much more of a flavour of the person. So, use some 'I' language from time to time, show that you are there behind the facts.

It can be quite difficult sometimes to think of positive words, and you can end up repeating 'enjoy' several times. Here are some alternatives:

- enthusiastic about
- pleased with/about
- enthusiasm for
- keen on
- passion for
- eager to
- interest in
- excited about
- fascination for
- stimulated by
- attracted to
- delighted with/to/by
- curious about
- happy about
- like
- exhilarated by/about
- committed to
- vision for
- sympathetic to
- skilled in.

Likewise, you can present your words positively by using the present tense. Simply the difference between: *'served customers and stocked* shelves' and 'serve customers and stock shelves.' A small point, but somehow the present tense sounds more dynamic and appealing.

Activity

Now that you have your list of interests and have considered how to make them sound really positive, write them into one or two sentences. Practise until you are confident they will appeal to a shortlister.

Remember, though, that you may have to rework this section to fit the requirements of different jobs.

Evidence of success

If you are at the very early stages of your career employers will not expect these successes to be world shattering, but it's still important to include them. You need to ask yourself in relation to each skill: *'What evidence can I provide to prove my success in this area?'*

You do this by thinking in terms of *measurable* skills, abilities and achievements. For example: how many words can you type a minute, software packages can you use, people can you serve in a day, or items can you sort in an hour?

Also, how much money did you save or earn for the organisation, or time did you save by making that time-saving suggestion? You may even have something to write about what percentage of total sales you made, how quickly you delivered the newspapers, the number of 'thank-you' letters you received, how quickly you learned the systems, etc.

Here are some other examples:

'I built the scenery for the last two school plays.'

'My fund-raising efforts for the charity reached £2000.'

'I reorganised the layout of the college magazine, and sales increased by 5%.'

'I reorganised the way the goods were processed through the stores department and this saved the company £3000 a year.'

'The experiment I undertook in chemistry highers was later written up for the school magazine.'

'In two years I didn't miss a single day working at my Saturday job.'

'I was the supermarket champion for spotting people trying to pass stolen credit cards.'

If you are applying for a university place then this sort of information becomes part of your 'Personal statement'. The same would be true for an application form. For a CV, you can add this as the 'something special' in relation to a particular job or course, writing at the bottom of your bullet-pointed list (Chapter four gives more detail on how to present this).

Special responsibilities

Have you held any special responsibilities at school, college, work or in your social life? These might include:

- being a prefect
- chairing meetings
- working on a committee
- being on working parties.

Activity

Make a note of any extra points you can include on your application form or CV. Try to present the information in a measurable format. The information below will give you ideas:

- teaching others
- helping at events
- being a monitor
- looking after others
- producing a play
- organising a special event
- escorting guests around the school/college.

Again, many of these items suggest that you have that something extra, over and above the run-of-the-mill person. Additionally, many of them suggest skills that may well be transferable to the job or course you seek.

Commendations, prizes and awards

Employers love achievers. If you've been an achiever in the past it shows you're motivated and will probably achieve in the future. Examples of this type of achievement might be the Queen's Guide or Queen's Scout Award, the Duke of Edinburgh Award, being head girl or boy, or receiving an award for the best dissertation.

Do mention them, even if they are not directly relevant, because they say something about the sort of person you are. They suggest that you are:

- more motivated than most people

- more hardworking than most people

- more academic than most people

- or, more conscientious than most people

... and that can't be a bad thing.

Publications

If you have ever had anything printed that you have written, mention it. People are always impressed. It doesn't have to be published in a magazine or newspaper. Maybe you had an article in your school or college magazine. Maybe you wrote guidelines on a particular procedure in the workplace. Maybe you wrote an information leaflet.

Where you place this information on your application form or CV will depend on how relevant it is to the course or job you are applying for. Looking at university applications first, if the published material is very pertinent to the course, weave a mention of it into the body of your text. If not, you might add it as a brief sentence at the end of your text.

The same rule generally applies to application forms. If there is nowhere to write it but it's important to mention, do so in the covering letter. For CVs the situation is different. Make a new heading, 'Articles published' or 'Publications' and list each there. You should give the following information across one line of text for each article:

- title of article/book/publication

- where published

- when published.

For example: 'Training methods', *Training Monthly*, July 2007

If it is not clear from the title, add a very brief explanation of the context of the publication, for example: 'Training methods' – an overview of the variety of methods available to the trainer when designing a course.

Activity

Make a note of any special achievements, responsibilities, awards or publications that you want to mention on an application form or CV. Use the following words:

Positive words to show experience and/or achievement

accomplished	achieved	adapted	administered	advanced
analysed	applied	assessed	benefited	built
challenged	combined	communicated	compiled	completed
conceived	conducted	controlled	coordinated	converted
created	delivered	demonstrated	designed	developed
devised	diagnosed	directed	economical	effective
efficient	eliminated	enabled	encouraged	enhanced
established	evolved	exceeded	excelled	expanded
experienced	extended	formulated	fulfilled	gained
generated	guided	identified	implemented	improved
incorporated	increased	influenced	initiated	innovative
instigated	integrated	introduced	launched	led
managed	minimised	monitored	motivated	mounted
organised	participated	perfected	performed	persuaded
prepared	produced	proficient	profitable	progressed
promoted	proposed	qualified	quantified	raised
recovered	redesigned	reorganised	repaired	resolved
resourceful	restored	revitalised	secured	simplified
sold	solved	specialised	stimulated	strengthened
successful	supervised	terminated	trained	transformed

Overcoming common problems

Golden rules

It is fairly rare for anyone to be able to look at an advertisement for a job (or a job description) and be able to say, 'This was written for me!' In this section we will look at how to get around the lack of ideal fit between what the employer wants and what you've got. But first of all, two golden rules.

The first one is, if you really like the look of a job, go for it even if it appears that you are less than ideal. This is particularly true when unemployment is low. What have you got to lose? Even if you waste time completing an application form or CV just to be rejected, you can use the work you put in for the next application. One thing you soon learn is that completing application forms can quickly become a chore. So working on one is never wasted, because you can copy or adapt what you've written for the next form you complete.

The second rule is to minimise your problem. Give the information you must provide, but don't emphasise the gaps. For example, what's the point in actually saying (perhaps in your covering letter) 'I know I don't have the .... you require, but am very interested in this job'. Let the reader find out by looking at your form. Never point out the undesirable.

Too young

It's sadly true that we live in an ageist society. However, there is now legislation against ageism in the workplace, and employers should be shortlisting you against your skills and competencies alone.

Too inexperienced

You may have heard of the expression 'catch-22'. Basically, it means when you are in a no-win situation. Being too inexperienced is often a catch-22 situation. You can't get the experience without the job, and you can't get the job without the experience. Stalemate. However, all is not lost.

Earlier in this chapter you were asked to list all your skills and personal qualities. You then went on to consider those skills you have that may be transferable. Look back to see how you worked out your transferable skills. Mentioning these transferable skills may help you to overcome the catch-22 situation.

Health problems

There are no strict guidelines for disclosing health problems. There are, however, some which are 'traditionally' mentioned on application forms. These are health problems like epilepsy, and physical disabilities that may affect the way a job is done. Some other complaints, such as diabetes or slight hearing or visual problems, are 'invisible' and you should use your judgement about whether to mention them. This judgement could be based on the type of work you are applying for and the extent of your disability. If you have a more serious disability speak to staff at your Jobcentre Plus for advice.

There is legislation against discrimination (the Disability Discrimination Act (DDA)), and employers have a duty to employ you if you are the best candidate for the job and they can do so with 'reasonable adaptation' to building or equipment or with you having a helper.

The DDA Helpline provides information and advice about all aspects of the DDA, and can advise on specialist organisations to contact if necessary. It also offers practical advice on employment for disabled people. Their website is http://www.direct.gov.uk/DisabledPeople/fs/en

Also, some employers belong to what's called the 'Green Tick' scheme. This means that they guarantee to interview anyone with a disability who meets the essential criteria they have stated are necessary for the job.

Wrong qualifications

One of the really tough things about our education system is that we have to make choices about which subjects to take, at a time when most of us haven't a clue what we want to do with our lives. This can mean that the choices we made at age 14 can affect our chances of achieving the goals we set ourselves at age 16, 18 or 20. Well, unfortunately, we can't turn back the clock, so we have to work with what we've got.

If you are thinking of applying for a college place in a different subject area, ask yourself 'How can I sell this 'odd' application to the college?' Let's therefore imagine that you took all science subjects at school, but now want to do an arts course. Why? How can you really convince the reader that this is an abiding interest and not just a passing whim? Can your head teacher, or whoever writes the letter to your college, back up your application with examples?

For some subjects it would be very unlikely that you could get a place without prior learning, and science would be one of these. Can you apply to a college that has an introductory year of some sort in your chosen subject area?

By the way, this is another situation where simply getting older helps. Many colleges and universities are much more relaxed about entry qualifications for older students, believing that they have the self-knowledge and motivation to study hard and see the course through.

If you are applying for a job that specifies different qualifications to your own, many of the same points apply. How can you convince the prospective interviewer that, despite the 'wrong' qualifications, you have sufficient knowledge and skills to handle the job? Do you have valuable experience if not the qualifications? Do you have similar, transferable skills? In times of high unemployment there are likely to be many people with the 'right' qualifications applying for a job, but remember 'nothing ventured nothing gained'. You definitely won't get the job if you don't apply for it. If unemployment is low, employers can't afford to be so choosy and you will stand a much better chance.

A murky past?

Do you have any skeletons in your cupboard? Did you, for example: get excluded from school for cheating in an exam; skip lot of classes; get in trouble with the law; job hop for the past two years; get sacked from your last job; have a reputation for laziness?

Well, if you can answer 'yes' to any of these types of question, the next question has to be, 'Does anyone have to know?'. The answer is: it depends on the sort of course or job you are applying for.

If you got excluded, or truanted a lot, for example, it may be mentioned in any letter or reference from your school, and there is little you can do about that. However, if you are genuinely a reformed character and have had time to prove it, you could ask the teacher either not to mention earlier problems, or to say how your situation and behaviour have improved.

For some jobs trouble with the law won't count, but with others they're vitally important. If you helped your dad with a bullion raid, a bank might think twice about you. Agencies working with children would definitely not look at you if you had a history of abusing children. You should never lie on an application form or CV. But remember, some questions simply aren't asked at the paper stage, and it is up to the interviewer to ask those questions at the interview itself. If you do have to write about these issues and they are part of your 'youthful indiscretion', as it is called, you may want to point out that you've grown up a bit since then, and are keen to be successful in your chosen course or career. Again, see if you can get someone who will give you a reference that will confirm this. Many employers understand that teenagers occasionally do daft things and, as long as they think you have changed for the better, they will often overlook minor problems.

'We realise that a lot of young people do silly things and get themselves into trouble. As long as it's nothing serious, and they show they are reformed characters, we will overlook it.'

Quote from the head of a building company

Overcoming prejudice

There are some fairly common prejudices, and these are usually based around easily observable differences. People are often fearful of others they see as in some way different. These differences include ethnic origin, gender, religion, sexuality, age, disability, politics, class, accent or lifestyle.

In Great Britain there is currently legislation against discrimination on the grounds of gender, race, disability, religion, sexuality and age. This means that these are the only areas where you will have legal backing if you can prove discrimination. And proving such discrimination is a problem in itself.

The difficulty is that unless you know the person opening your envelope, you don't know if you are dealing with a prejudiced person or not. I prefer to be optimistic and trust that people are fair. However, this is not always the case. All of which leaves you with the need to make a decision about how to handle prejudice. Do you have a foreign-sounding name? Are you are female applying for work in a traditionally male job market, or vice versa? How can you handle this? You could consider not mentioning your religion or political beliefs in the 'Additional information' section, or you could use only initials instead of your first name on your application form or CV. In fact, many equal opportunities employers only ask for this. And, if it is relevant, you could avoid including interests that indicate your sexuality or lifestyle if these might be considered 'alternative'.

Of course, you shouldn't have to do any of these things, but you may decide to play safe.

'I can't believe how many interviewers still ask questions like 'Are you planning to have children?'. This is the type of question that could lead to them being taken to a tribunal.'

Quote from a recruitment specialist

If you are absolutely sure that you are being discriminated against, you can take your case up with either:

Commission for Racial Equality

St Dunstan's House, 201-211 Borough High Street, London SE1 1GZ. Tel: 020 7939 0000. Fax: 020 7939 0001. Email info@cre.gov.uk or one of their local offices. You can find their details on their website www.cre.gov.uk

or, for gender issues for Great Britain:

Equal Opportunities Commission

Arndale House, Arndale Centre, Manchester M4 3EQ. Tel: 0845 601 5901. Fax: 0161 838 1733. Email: info@eoc.org.uk. Website: www.eoc.org.uk

or, for Scotland:

St Stephens House, 279 Bath Street, Glasgow G2 4JL. Tel: 0845 601 5901. Fax: 0141 248 5834. Email: scotland@eoc.org.uk

or, for Wales:

Windsor House, Windsor Lane, Cardiff CF10 3GE. Tel: 0845 601 5901. Fax: 029 2064 1079.

or, for disability:

DRC Helpline

Freepost, MIDO 2064, Stratford-upon-Avon CV37 9BR. Tel: 08457 622 633. Textphone: 08457 622 644. Fax: 08457 778 878. Website: www.drc-gb.org/whatwedo/helplineservices.asp

Disabled applicants can also get help from Jobcentre Plus. Website: www.jobcentreplus.gov.uk

There is also legislation against discrimination on the grounds of sexuality, age and religion. You can easily find more details on the internet.

Chapter checklist

This chapter has been about analysing what you have to offer a potential employer. Do you now know:

- the skills you have to offer
- your positive personal qualities
- what positive achievements you can discuss
- what makes you stand out from the crowd
- how you would describe yourself
- what you would say are your strengths
- what your weaknesses are and how you will overcome them
- how you can sell your interests to best effect
- what to do if you think you are being discriminated against?

Chapter three

How managers shortlist

You should read this chapter:

- before you begin to complete your application form or write your CV.

By the end of the chapter you should know:

- the mechanisms that shortlisters use to select candidates for interview
- some tips for making it easy for shortlisters to select you for interview.

Think like a shortlister

When you are completing your application form or writing a CV for a job, it is really helpful to know how managers shortlist. By doing this, you can anticipate what they are looking for and make sure you provide it.

In large organisations there is often a personnel or human resource specialist who guides managers through the recruitment process. Either alone, or with the manager, they will select the applicants to be shortlisted for interview.

However, it is true that in many organisations there is no one with specialist knowledge of recruitment, and many shortlisters are not trained. This means they may not follow the procedures in this chapter. But take heart. By following these guidelines you will still give yourself the best chance of being shortlisted.

What follows is how good shortlisters operate. It can't take into account the individual peculiarities of untrained people. Increasingly, though, organisations are using procedures such as those described in this chapter because it can save them from being seen as unfair and perhaps taken to an industrial tribunal. They will often keep the notes on how they shortlisted and on the interview for six months, in case of later challenges.

By the way, this means that if you are not shortlisted when you expected to be, you could contact the organisation and ask why. This may be useful information to help you when you apply for your next job.

'I have just been reading through a batch of application forms for an administrative post. Not one person knew how to properly complete the section, 'Give further evidence in support of your application.'

Quote from a manager at Cambridge University

Job descriptions, person specifications and competencies

When managers are shortlisting, they base their choice on *selection criteria*. These criteria show how what you have said about yourself matches what they are looking for in a successful candidate. The selection criteria are often provided by companies. If provided you must study them carefully. The criteria are usually to be found in the job description and the person specification for that job. Some organisations also judge you against criteria called competencies, sometimes known as *behaviours*.

Chapter four explains in more detail the differences between the three.

But briefly:

- a *job description* describes the tasks the person has to do

- a *person specification* describes the person who could do those tasks

- a *competency* is the behaviour the worker will be displaying when they are performing a task correctly.

For example, the task on the job description could be 'type manager's letters', and the corresponding item on the person specification could be 'able to type at 45 wpm'. The competency would be something like 'Completes all typing on time and to the required standard'. Sometimes items in the person specification will have 'essential' or 'desirable' written beside them.

So when shortlisters are reading through a pile of application forms or CVs, their task is quite mechanical. They are looking for someone who has the skills, personality and competencies identified to do the job well – in other words meet the criteria they set. Some employers concentrate on both the job description and the person specification to help them do this, others rely much more heavily on the person specification. Yet others use both of these, plus the competencies. In fact any of these three alone or in any combination is possible.

To make sure you get shortlisted it is therefore important to look at the selection criteria if they are provided. Some organisations will tell you what their selection criteria are: that is, if they include the job description, person specification, competencies or any combination of these three. If they don't, look at Chapter four, which shows you how to work out what would be in them if you had them.

To help managers to shortlist they will have a grid something like this:

Candidate name:		Vacancy:	
Criteria	Met	Partly met	Not met
Type manager's correspondence			
Deal with callers to the office			
Answer the phone			
Deal with customer queries			
File accurately			

Sometimes they may use numbers:

	Smith	Jones	Patel	Wisby
Essential				
Type at 45 wpm				
GCSE English				
GCSE maths				
Customer service skills				
Desirable				
Competent user of PowerPoint				
Basic knowledge of Excel				
Scoring: 1 = not mentioned, 2 = poor match, 3 = good match, 4 = exceptional match				

As they read through your information, they simply tick one of the boxes or decide a score. The people with the highest score or most ticks in the 'met' or 'partly met' boxes get shortlisted. This means that you should always present information about yourself in the same order as is shown in the criteria. This is true for both CVs and application forms. Make it easy for the shortlister to choose you.

'Candidates have no idea how long it takes to shortlist when they present their information in a haphazard way. If they get it right, they're well ahead of the field.'

Quote from a pharmaceutical company manager

Activity

Look at an advertisement for a job that interests you. Alternatively, phone the organisation for a job description and person specification or find them on the web. Now think about the skills, knowledge and attributes you could offer the employer. Imagine that you are shortlisting. How many of the items mentioned could you meet to gain a 'met' or 'partly met' mark or a good score? Tip – don't be put off because you can't meet all the items. Even if you can only meet some, go for the job if you really want it – others will be in the same position as yourself. What have you got to lose?

Chapter checklist

Shortlisters who are trained will follow good practice when selecting candidates for interview. They will:

- use the job description, person specification and/or competencies in combination as the basis for their selection. These are their *selection criteria*

- have designed a shortlisting grid to judge what you write about yourself against the selection criteria

- use the shortlisting form to assess and record your suitability for the job.

Chapter four

Dazzling CVs – key contents

You should read this chapter:

- when you need to prepare a CV for either a specific job or for a general mailing to a number of organisations.

By the end of this chapter you should know:

- what a CV is

- the advantages and disadvantages of this method of presenting information about yourself

- how to use advertisements, job descriptions, person specifications and competencies to help you to construct your CV

- about CV templates on your PC and electronic CVs.

What is a CV?

The term CV is an abbreviation for curriculum vitae, which means 'the course of your life' – although employers will only be interested in your life as it relates to the job they have to offer. Sometimes CVs are called résumés.

Advantages and disadvantages of the CV

Advantages

Because there is no single right way to present a CV, and because so many people do it poorly, it gives you an opportunity to shine over the opposition if you make a good job of yours. Also, unlike when you are completing application forms, when you write a CV it is you who decides what to include. And because you choose the CV headings yourself, you can have a separate heading for any unusual work or academic information you wish to present. This is especially useful if you want to emphasise any particular points. For example, I always have a separate heading for 'Publications'. Again, because you choose the headings yourself, you can miss out any information you prefer not to include. This information might include periods of unemployment or poor examination results.

CV preparation is an excellent way of training your mind to present information succinctly. This may be of real help to you when preparing for an interview. The CV is an excellent 'crib sheet' if you are invited to interview. It will help you to think through what you could be asked about.

Disadvantages

It can feel as if you have to make the whole thing up from scratch each time. Actually, when you have done the work once, you will only need to revise it rather than rewrite it in future, because the bulk of the work will be done and you can cut and paste much of the information into future versions of your CV.

CVs leave little space for the sort of wider discussion of your abilities you can sometimes provide on the blank space on application forms headed 'Information in support of your application' or similar.

You really need to use a typewriter or wordprocessor to produce a well-presented CV. However, it is much more acceptable to complete an application form by hand, especially if using a wordprocessor makes it more difficult to fit the information into the boxes allocated on the form.

'One of the things I like about a CV rather than an application form is that it allows me to present myself in exactly the way I like. I can be much more imaginative.'

Quote from an applicant

CV style

Chapter five gives you a lot of information about style, and you need to read that in conjunction with this chapter. However, here are a few additional points.

Good presentation

Your CV should be wordprocessed. This makes it easier to make alterations or move text around. You can vary the font size and type. You have a thesaurus and spell checker to assist you and can even check your grammar. And, bearing in mind that you should adapt your CV for each job, the best point about using a wordprocessor is the ease with which you can do this.

Fonts

But don't use too many fonts on the same document or it will look messy (three is generally considered the maximum). Also, don't go crazy with font sizes: be consistent in what you use for what information and don't use a font that is difficult to read.

Most people use one of three fonts:

- **Comic Sans MS** – this is very popular at the moment and looks very up to date

- **Times New Roman** – was one of the most popular until recently, still very commonly used

- **Arial** – another popular choice.

Emphasising information

Don't use too many different ways of emphasising information. Your choice is underlining, or making text bold, or making text italicised, or altering text size. Remember to be consistent with how you use these ways of emphasising points.

There is more information about CV layout in Chapter five.

CV content

Even more important than the style and layout of your CV is the content. We need to consider what you want to present to a prospective employer. Initially, we'll assume you are preparing a CV in response to a particular job advertisement, rather than just sending CVs out 'uninvited' (some tips on dealing with 'on spec' CVs will be covered in Chapter five).

To do this you need to gather together before you start:

- the information you noted about yourself
- the advertisement
- the selection criteria (usually the job description, person specification, competencies or any combination of these)
- any other information you have about the organisation
- plenty of scrap paper (or a new file on your wordprocessor).

Let me take you back a step in case you are not clear about some of the terms.

A *job description* describes the job to be done. This usually consists of a list of the main tasks involved in the work. Some employers write alongside each task the percentage of time spent on that task or sometimes indicate how important each task is. Most employers also have a final 'catch-all' heading along the lines of 'and anything else your manager tells you to do'!

A *person specification* describes the person who can do the job. This will be a list of personal and professional attributes the employer is looking for in the postholder. It is very common for this list to be split in some way into 'essential' and 'desirable' qualities. When looking through all the application forms or CVs, the employer will be looking for people who can meet all, or at least most, of the 'essential' requirements. If there are several or many of these, the employer will then seek out those applicants who also have as many as possible of the 'desirable' qualities.

Competencies (sometimes called *behaviours*) are the behaviours the worker will be showing when working effectively.

So, as mentioned in Chapter three, someone looking for a wordprocessing operator might have *'type all correspondence for three managers'* in the job description list (this describes the task to be done, and identifies clearly the skills the person needs to have). In the person specification list it would read something like *'able to type at 45 wpm'*. The competency might be *'works to required standard'.*

Selection criteria

One or more of the documents mentioned above (job description, person specification and competencies) are almost certainly going to be what employers are judging your application against. These will then be the *selection criteria*. It is vitally important that your CV (or application form) is targeted closely at these criteria.

What to do if you are not supplied with selection criteria

You may have applied for the job, but not been sent any selection criteria or any information about the organisation. If so, you need to do some basic detective work. Tips on how to deal with this situation are given below.

Phone the organisation and ask if they can provide you with any of these documents. If they can't, and you are unclear exactly what the job will involve, ask if you can speak to the human resources (sometimes called personnel) manager, or whoever is dealing with the vacancy, to get more details. Remember when you do this that you need to sound polished and confident, because the conversation (as well as your CV) might affect your chances of an interview.

If this is still not possible, phone your local Connexions service or Jobcentre Plus office to see if they can give you any clues. They may not be able to help with the person specification, but will almost certainly be able to give you some ideas about what the type of job might involve. They are also likely to know something about most employers in your region, especially if they have used the Jobcentre Plus service to fill a vacancy.

Look for further information about the organisation. This may be:

- word of mouth – find out what other people know about them

- by keeping an eye on the local press

- by looking in the national press – or on the internet if it's a big organisation

- by looking in trade or professional journals (your main library will probably have them)

- by looking on the web.

From this basic information you can work out for yourself what the person specification is likely to include. Later in this chapter there are a couple of job descriptions and person specifications that will give you a further idea of the connection between the two.

Working out the selection criteria

If you aren't provided with the selection criteria try to work out for yourself what might be in it by using the information you have gathered. That way you can focus the information you provide more meaningfully. You can make a reasonably intelligent guess and probably pick up most of the main points. Here is one example to show you how to do it. We'll start with the advertisement, which will give you some valuable information.

NIGHT SHIFT WORKER

MACHINE OPERATOR

Tasty Bread Products Ltd are seeking three additional night shift workers to help produce our high-quality bread products.

Applicants should have good health and have good general education. Full training given, although experience of this type of work would be an advantage.

Basic pay £XXX for a 41-hour week, four weeks' annual holiday and good working conditions.

For details, contact:

Mrs Singh, Tasty Bread Products Ltd

Broomfield Road, Manchester M12 3RR

Tel: 01762 410679

Now look at the job description:

TASTY BREAD PRODUCTS LTD

JOB DESCRIPTION

MACHINE OPERATOR

Machine operators are accountable to the production supervisor, Mr G. Smith.

The main tasks of the job are to:

1. ensure that the correct ingredients are added to machines to guarantee production to the correct standards

2. follow the progress of the mixture to the next stage of processing

3. ensure hygiene standards are achieved

4. make adjustments to the machine as necessary to ensure smooth operation

5. report any faults

6. clean the machine at the end of the shift.

Now you've got a wealth of information.

Activity

Carefully read through the advertisement on the previous page and job description above, and underline any words that you think are important.

Do not read any further until this activity is complete.

Now, what sort of person would they be looking for to undertake this type of work? (This tells you what they would put in a person specification and competencies.)

The points I feel are important are embolded below:

1. ensure that the **correct ingredients** are added to machines to guarantee production to the correct standards

2. **follow the progress** of the mixture to the next stage of processing

3. ensure **hygiene standards** are achieved

4. make **adjustments** to the machine as necessary to ensure smooth operation

5. **report any faults**

6. **clean** the machine at the end of the shift.

Now, what sort of person would they be looking for to undertake this type of work?

Here are some factors that might well be included in the person specification and the list of competencies.

1. The emphasis on correct ingredients suggests a need for attention to detail.

2. The person must be observant in order to ensure that the mixture is progressing satisfactorily (and also to note whether the machine is operating properly).

3. The person must be clean and tidy in order to maintain hygiene standards.

4. The person must be thorough in order to clean the machine properly (food manufacturers can incur huge fines if their machinery is dirty).

5. The person must be able to use their own initiative to decide whether to try to fix a fault him/herself or to report it to someone else.

I am sure that this working environment would also be one where people would not be allowed to smoke.

There you have it. Knowing nothing about food production techniques (as indeed you may not if it's your first job and you've no prior knowledge), I've made a reasonably intelligent guess at the selection criteria for a machine operator. So the finished person specification might look something like the table opposite.

'I spend a lot of time working on a CV, usually several hours spread over two or three days. It's absolutely vital to adapt each CV to the job you're applying for. It must work – I always get invited to interview.'

Quote from an employee

PERSON SPECIFICATION

MACHINE OPERATOR

E = Essential D = Desirable

The person appointed to this post must be:

1. fit and healthy **E**

2. attentive to detail **E**

3. observant **E**

4. clean and tidy **E**

5. thorough in their approach to their work **E**

6. able to use initiative **E**

7. reliable **E**

8. experienced in this type of work **D**

And the list of competencies might be something like:

- able to use own initiative
- takes a pride in own work
- willing to admit mistakes and not blame others
- willing to learn
- able to work with minimal supervision after training period is completed
- thinks creatively about how to solve problems.

'Some CVs make me laugh. All the vacancies I advertise for require attention to detail, yet I receive CVs with spelling mistakes, poor grammar and other errors. The candidate is hardly demonstrating that they can do what I'm asking.'

Quote from a manager in a research organisation

Now it's your turn.

Activity

Here is an advertisement and, on the next page, a job description for a training officer. Using the same process, work out the likely person specification and competencies.

STAFF TRAINING OFFICER
Housing and Social Services

We are looking for a suitably qualified graduate to join our small lively team involved in developing our human resources.

Broxbridge has a high commitment to staff development. New legislation, alterations in the structure of the department and changes in working practices mean that we seek an additional training officer to assist in staff training in a wide range of subjects. We seek someone with human resources qualifications, and preferably with some training experience.

Send a CV to:

Ms. D. Jones, Human Resource Manager
Broxbridge Borough Council
Room 114
Central Block
High Street
Broxbridge L11 T56

BROXBRIDGE BOROUGH COUNCIL
STAFF TRAINING OFFICER
JOB DESCRIPTION

Responsible to: Staff Group Training Manager

Scale: Grade C

Main purpose of job

The Staff Training Officer is responsible to the Staff Group Training Manager for assisting Senior Staff Training Officers in the provision of training and development for all members of staff.

Duties

1. To analyse the training and development needs of individual members of staff and staff groups.

2. To assist in the design and delivery of appropriate training courses and development strategies to meet these needs.

3. To identify training provided out of house and to keep staff informed of such opportunities.

4. To evaluate the effectiveness of training provided both internally and externally.

5. To stock and catalogue a library of resource material for the training department.

6. To undertake any other duties as identified by the Staff Group Training Manager.

Reflection

How did you get on? Did you consider general issues that you might have known from simply being aware of what's going on around you? For example, as well as more obvious items, the person specification and/ or competencies for this particular job are likely to include something about a commitment to equal opportunities and cultural inclusiveness training, and the candidate being prepared to work in a non-smoking environment. Because these are the requirements of many councils, it makes sense to slip these details in somewhere on your CV. Even if they are not on the actual person specification or competencies, they would be welcomed.

Just to remind you – person specifications are usually divided into 'essential' and 'desirable' qualities. If you do have to write your own person specification, try to work out which would be which and ensure that you try to prove that you can meet at least the essential requirements. But again, don't be put off applying just because you don't have everything.

OK, so now you have all that you need to get down to work. Let's start with the easy bit.

Biographical details

There are certain facts about you that you should always include on a CV. These are:

- your full name

- your full address, including postcode

- your telephone number, including the area code; mobile number; email address, if you have one.

There are two schools of thought about including your date of birth. Employers *must not* take this into account as ageism is illegal. It's up to you to decide whether to include it or not.

Layout of factual details

Here is an example of how to present this information:

Philipa Rudinsky
123 Peterson Road
Walmsley
Lancs WM2 3ER
01333 678903   07878 654987
p.rudinsky@tto.com

Health

You don't need to state your health on your CV if you would prefer not to, but you will almost certainly be asked about this on an application form. If you have good health, state 'excellent' (anything less, even 'good', and people will think there is something wrong). The section on 'Overcoming common problems' in Chapter two discusses in more detail how to present health difficulties that need to be disclosed.

Nationality

Some people also add details of nationality. Legally, employers must be confident that you are able to work in this country and should ask at interview to see your passport, birth certificate or work visa. However, on your CV you can choose whether or not to add nationality. If you think that your nationality may lead to unfair discrimination, leave it out.

Marital status

It is not common to put your marital status on a CV, because in some cases it can lead to unfair discrimination. I recommend you leave this out.

Professional profile statement

At the beginning of your CV, immediately below your name and address section, you should write a punchy professional profile statement. This is a brief statement about yourself that lets the reader have a really powerful idea of the person you are and makes them think, *'Yes! This person I want to see!'*

This is where you sell all those aspects of your personality that make you so great to employ. You've already given evidence of them, now's your chance to name them and sell them blatantly.

If you have any work experience your statement should start by stating who you are in work terms – 'Efficient secretary', 'Experienced machine worker', and so on. Then you write about personality traits, very important to employees. In his book *Hiring the Best* (Thorsons, 1988), John Martin Yates lists the 17 personality traits of a successful employee. Many of the items in this list are the types of qualities that would be on an employer's list of competencies. Here they are:

Personal traits

Drive: has a desire to get things done; is goal- rather than task-oriented; has an ability to make decisions and to avoid 'busy work'; breaks overwhelming tasks into their component parts.

Motivation: looks for new challenges; has enthusiasm and a willingness to ask questions; can motivate others through their own interests in doing a good job.

Communication: can talk and write to people at all levels (an increasingly important skill).

Chemistry: does not get rattled and point the finger of blame; wears a smile; has confidence without self-importance; is cooperative with others; demonstrates leadership by an ability to draw a team together.

Energy: always gives that extra effort in the small things as well as the important tasks.

Determination: does not back off when the going gets tough; has the ability to cope; can be assertive when necessary; is, at the same time, shrewd enough to know when it is time to back off.

Confidence: is not ostentatious; is poised, friendly, honest with all employees, high and low, yet knows when to keep a secret.

'I recently shortlisted for a secretarial job. I couldn't believe the poor quality of the CVs. For example, one applicant was a researcher at a university and she had sent in her normal researcher's CV, which had no relevance whatsoever to the job she was applying for. It was a waste of her time and mine.'

Quote from the manager of a local authority

Professional traits

Reliability: follows up on self; does not rely on others to ensure that a job is well done; keeps management informed.

Integrity: takes responsibility for own actions, whether good or bad; makes decisions in the best interests of the company, not on their own whim or personal preference.

Dedication: has a commitment to tasks and projects; does what is necessary to see a project through to completion on deadline.

Pride: has pride in trade or profession; takes the extra step and always pays attention to details to see the job is done to the best of ability.

Analytical skills: weighs up the pros and cons; does not jump at the first solution that presents itself; analyses the short- and long-term benefits of a solution against all its possible negatives; possesses the perception and insight that lead to good judgement.

Listening skills: listens and understands rather than waits for a chance to speak; has attentiveness that complements analytical skills.

Business traits

Efficiency: always keeps an eye open for wastes of time, effort, resources and money.

Economy: knows the difference between expensive and cheap solutions to problems; spends your money as if it were his or her own.

Procedures: knows that procedures usually exist for good reason, and won't work around them; has a willingness to keep you informed; follows the chain of command; does not implement own 'improved' procedures or organise others to do so.

Profit: knows it's the reason we're all here.

Activity

1. Make a list of the personality traits that you think apply to you and what examples you can provide if you get to interview. Keep in mind that much of your evidence will be amply demonstrated by the 'noteworthy extras' that are listed above. However, it is possible that you can give an example from some other area of your CV, such as the interests section.

2. Think about those traits you would like to develop. What steps can you take to achieve them? Write a step-by-step approach to make sure you develop and keep these traits.

Here is a handy format for writing your profile

'A ... (describe your first personality quality using an adjective) ... (second positive personality adjective)... (describe your present situation, e.g. student or job title),... with strong/ excellent/outstanding/exceptional skills in ... (skill area). My experience has provided me with the following strengths:

- *strength one*
- *strength two*
- *strength three*
- *strength four*
- *strength five*
- *strength six.'*

As in the format above, you can follow up this profile with some bullet points highlighting your strengths. Add a sentence that says something like *'I also have the following strengths, skills and qualities'* or *'My career to date has given me the following strengths, abilities and qualities'.* Follow this with six or eight bullet points (dots, stars, or whatever) emphasising these aspects of your abilities.

Here is an example of a professional profile prepared by an applicant for the training officer job we looked at earlier:

Staff and Management Development Professional. I work well with staff at all levels. Energetic and enthusiastic; I have experience in running a wide range of staff development courses. I am also computer literate, competent on several software packages. Additionally, I can offer the following competencies:

- creative solutions to training needs
- attention to detail
- conscientious
- value diversity
- team player
- able to use own initiative.

Education and training information

There are actually two headings here – 'education' and 'training'. Depending on your own circumstances you might choose to separate the information or put them together under different headings.

Whichever way you choose, here are a few tips to help you present the information in the best possible way.

Education information

Education information consists of three groups of information – where you attended school/college/university, when, and the qualifications you obtained.

- No employer is likely to be interested in details of your primary school so don't include this information.
- Don't give the whole address of your secondary school or college; simply 'St John's School, Bradford' is enough.

- Remember to be consistent in the way you present information.
- If you are writing a list of, say, exam passes, put the most relevant ones at the top.

The higher up the educational ladder you go, the less you need to mention lower qualifications, so if you:

- only have five GCSEs mention each one separately (also, if you are a school-leaver you would normally add the grades you achieved – though if they are poor you might want to omit them)
- have a degree, you probably wouldn't bother to list your GCSEs – unless there was a good reason to do so.

Here is an example of how to present education information:

Jennifer Ann Peters

26 Sunningdale Road
Marsham
Norfolk
NR2 6AS

01990 575849

Schools attended:

2005–2007 Berne Community College, Marsham

1998–2005 St Mary's School, Oxford

Qualifications

2007   GCE A level: English B, sociology C, media studies A

2005   GCSE: English B, mathematics C, geography A, history C, art A, sociology B, technology and design C

Training information

The term training covers a multitude of different teaching methods. For example, you may have attended short courses or a longer course that were not certificated. You may have some NVQ or GNVQ units.

You could have done an Apprenticeship or attended an in-company course. Less formally, you could have been coached by other members of staff, spent time in different departments or attended evening classes.

Any, or all of these, are likely to be of interest to a potential employer.

Some people are course junkies and soon collect quite a long list. If this applies to you, be selective about which ones to include. Ignore courses that have no direct relevance to the job you are applying for. The link, by the way, could be that the course (perhaps recreational) highlights some personal characteristic that will be useful for the work. If so, try to spell this out, perhaps in the 'Additional information' section, or the reader may not understand the point.

Here are some tips about presenting 'training information'.

- List your courses in the best possible order – by relevance to the job and by standard.

- If the course title leaves the reader unclear as to its content, very briefly state what was included, perhaps by listing the modules.

- If the course is a long one but still did not lead to a qualification, state the length of the course or the reader may think it's just another short course.

- State where you did the course, but don't put the whole address, simply 'Cambridge Regional College' or 'Timeworks, London' will do.

Do remember to consider transferable skills when you are deciding which courses to include in your list. For example, suppose you worked in a shop and the company sent you on a 'customer service' course. The skills you learn on that course would be just as valuable if you became a sales representative, a customer services manager, work in a different type of shop, or indeed anywhere else where you have direct contact with customers.

Activity

Make a note of your education and training details. Remember to include date, school/college attended, brief address, qualification and grades (if appropriate). For training include course title, date, training organisation and content, if appropriate.

Work experience/career to date/career history

This section usually takes the longest to compose, because you are carefully matching your information against the items in the *selection criteria* (the job description, person specification and competencies, if these are provided) for the job. You will see that I have given three possible titles in this section heading – use whichever you prefer, or another similar one of your choice.

The prospective employer will read through the education section of your CV, and briefly note if you've got the right qualifications, but the career history section is the one they will scrutinise most closely. Therefore time taken here is well spent.

If you have worked your way through Chapter two, you will have already done most of the work needed. If you haven't, go back now and work through the material so that you have an accurate assessment of all your skills and competencies, and an idea of how to use words to best effect. Before you consider how to present this information, remember that it should be woven into the fabric of your work experience. There are a number of different ways to show work experience on a CV and we'll look at these later in the chapter.

When you are writing your 'career to date' section, weave into your statements those words that you have underlined as being significant in the selection criteria of the job you are applying for. This will work on the shortlister unconsciously, and help them to feel well disposed towards your application.

Activity

1. In your notebook, list all your work experience. Remember to include holiday jobs, part-time work, full-time work, voluntary work, work experience/shadowing.

2. Then, under each heading, note your dates – from start of employment to finish (month and year is sufficient).

3. Now take each of the jobs in turn and make a list of the responsibilities you held in the job. These are likely to be much the same as the job description, if you were given one at the time. Take into account any additional responsibilities – most jobs develop over time as the needs of the organisation or the interests of the employee shape them.

4. Now for each of these jobs ask yourself *'What did I do that was noteworthy?'*

'We read each candidate's CV again before they walk in for an interview. If the CV is well written and presented we are often more well disposed towards them.'

Quote from a manager of a charity

OK, so now you have job titles; factual details about them – dates, etc; responsibilities in each job; and noteworthy 'extras' for each job. Strictly speaking, that is all you need for the 'Career to date' section. As you list the responsibilities of each job, ensure that they are shown in the same order as in the selection criteria. This makes it easier for the shortlister to check that you meet their requirements. Remember to use some positive words.

An example of how to list the responsibilities of the job under the title is shown here:

2001–2004 Training Manager, Insurance Industries Ltd, Rotherham

In this busy post I have responsibility for:

- training and development needs of 650 staff
- successful analysis of training needs
- design and delivery of over 20 training courses, from two-hour to three-day
- appointing external trainers and other recruitment tasks
- detailed allocation of training budget.

Whilst in post I have completed an extensive training needs analysis and provided training linked to company objectives. All were within budget. I have also provided a library of management and related books for staff use. Staff attendance on courses has increased 15% during the last year.

Other information

As with the factual information, there is a choice of layouts and headings for the odds and ends you still want to include, but which haven't fitted neatly within any of the previous headings. Your information may fit into one of the following headings.

1. Leisure interests
2. Additional information
3. Publications
4. References

Leisure interests

It is more or less expected that you will include a section under this heading, although you may choose to use the heading 'Additional information' if that feels more appropriate (for example, if you want to include both leisure interests and information about one of the other items in this section). See Chapter two for more information on how to write this section.

Additional information

The type of additional information that may well interest a prospective employer (or a college or university) would be:

- membership of a club
- membership of a debating society
- extra responsibilities at school or college
- involvement with a charity or fundraising organisation
- playing sports
- voluntary work
- Duke of Edinburgh Award or similar.

Having said that, some of these activities may well provide you with experience that you can emphasise in the body of your CV.

If you decide to use one of the headings suggested above, don't just list the items. Think instead about what might interest the employer. Going through the above list I could easily identify the following.

- Membership of a club can indicate that you are a sociable person, or if the club is based around an interest or skill that you are good at whatever that is. It shows that you are not too much of a loner.

- Membership of a debating society indicates an ability to present yourself verbally, to think through issues logically and calmly.

- Extra responsibilities at school or college (for example, being a prefect) show that you are reliable, trustworthy, respected, etc.

- Playing sports shows that you are fit. Playing a team sport shows that you can work as a member of a team, play by the rules, etc.

- Voluntary work shows that you like to help others less fortunate than yourself, and shows reliability, initiative, etc.

- Duke of Edinburgh Award shows many positive attributes depending on what you've covered, but including staying power, reliability and willingness to work hard.

Providing this information to prospective employers is especially important if you are a school- or college-leaver with no work experience to offer as proof of your abilities. The types of qualities you will be discussing here are often related to the competencies all employers are interested in.

Publications

If you've been fortunate enough to have something published, no matter how modest the publication, do mention it. The format is: title, journal, publisher, date of publication.

Generally, the titles of articles are shown in plain type enclosed by quotation marks, and the titles of books are shown in italic type.

Maybe you haven't written a book or article but have written something else useful. Have you designed web pages, written an information leaflet, edited the school magazine? All of these would be of interest to an employer. If any relate directly to the type of work you are applying for, you may want to send a copy or give a brief description.

References

It is entirely up to you to decide whether or not to provide details of referees on your CV. If you are applying for a specific job, it is helpful to include this information, because some organisations insist on having the reference in front of them prior to the interview.

If, however, you are sending a CV out uninvited there is no need to include this information unless you particularly want to. The organisation can always ask for details of referees if they contact you for interview. When you do provide this information choose your referees carefully. You should select people who you feel have a good opinion of you, and who know something about you in the capacity you are seeking.

Do check with them that they will be willing to provide a reference. It sometimes happens that people get letters requesting a reference on someone they feel is totally unsuitable for the job in question, and this can be very embarrassing. Much better to check it out first. If the person agrees to provide a reference, do tell them about the job so that they have a chance to think about it ahead of time. Check too that they won't be away on holiday at the crucial time.

The information referees receive with the request varies. Some organisations simply ask referees to 'Write about the suitability of the person' without giving much guidance. Some ask referees to complete a form. Others send the selection criteria and ask for comments in relation to these documents. Others phone. It is usual to supply the names, addresses and telephone numbers of two referees. Obviously, if you have had a previous job, one of your referees should be your previous manager. If you have not had a previous job you could ask:

- a teacher from school or a lecturer from college
- a professional person who knows you well
- the chairperson or leader of a club you belong to
- a family friend who has a professional job.

If you are already employed and don't want your present employer to know that you are applying for other jobs, mention this in your covering letter (some application forms ask the question anyway). Simply say something like, 'Please do not contact my employer for a reference unless a job offer is to be made'.

Writing a CV to send out speculatively

So far we have been talking about CVs that are written specifically to apply for a particular job. You may decide that you want to send your CV to several organisations 'on spec'.

Many people hesitate to do this, but what have you got to lose but your time and the cost of the stationery and stamps? Remember, many organisations are delighted to be able to fill posts without the expense and trouble of advertising.

There are three approaches to sending out CVs speculatively.

- You send your CV to every organisation you can think of that may have a vacancy. This would work, for example, for a job as an office administrator – almost every organisation has some office staff.

- You send your CV to the types of organisation that may possibly have specific types of work – for example, all building companies in your area if you're looking for a bricklaying job.

- You send your CV to organisations that have been in the news and that you think may therefore have an opening in the future. This would be the case, for example, if you read that a company had won a big contract, is expanding, or has received an award. Anything positive, in fact, might be worth following with a CV and a covering letter. Chapter nine gives information on what to write in these circumstances.

The advantages of sending a CV 'on spec' are as follows.

- It shows the organisation that you are self motivated and can use your initiative.

- Even if there is not a vacancy at the moment, your information may be kept on file and the organisation may contact you if a vacancy arises.

- You may catch the organisation at a time when a vacancy has just arisen and they have not yet had an opportunity to advertise.

- You may contact the organisation when they are considering creating a new post – you'll be first in the queue.

- You could even find yourself being the only one interviewed because the organisation has not advertised the vacancy, which means that as long as you're good you don't have to worry about other interviewees who might be even better...

To sum up

- Think about the sort of work you want to apply for.

- Work out what the job entails and try to decide what the selection criteria might be.

- Write your CV as if you were writing to the organisation for that job.

- Under your name and contact details, on a separate line write 'Target job' (and state what it is) or 'Career goal' or similar.

- Write a suitable covering letter, indicating exactly the type of work you seek, or saying that you are open to suggestions. Alternatively, you could say that you are really looking for job 'X' but would be willing to consider others.

- Find out the name of the personnel or relevant manager, and send your letter and CV directly to that person (again, this shows initiative and will only cost a phone call).

- Consider following up your mailing with a phone call a few days later. If you do this, prepare beforehand for the call: what are you going to say? Make a few notes to ensure you handle the call well.

Activity

Investigate all the organisations in your area (or in the area in which you would like to live and work) that would have the type of vacancy you are looking for. Remember to find out to whom CVs should be sent.

Scannable CVs

Some organisations will scan your CV using specialist software. If they receive many applications this will save them time reading through all of them. They may request that you present your CV in a particular way, showing bare essentials, or they may scan the CV just as you send it.

The software will be looking for *key words or phrases* in your CV, chosen because they are considered most important to the potential postholder. Key words might include 'motivated', 'hardworking', 'good communicator', 'dynamic', etc. If you follow the advice given in this chapter, and ensure that you construct your CV in such a way that it includes key words from the selection criteria, you won't go far wrong. Take into account, also, John Martin Yate's key personality traits on page 69.

If you are asked for a scannable CV, but are not given a template, keep these points in mind.

1. Put your name at the top of each page on a line with nothing else on it.

2. Write all contact details on separate lines with no punctuation marks.

3. Use a single column format, as the scanning software will read from left to right.

4. Use bold or capitals for headings. Keep it simple: don't use borders, italics, underlining, shading or anything else that may confuse the scanner and prevent a good reading.

5. Use a sans serif font, such as Arial or Helvetica, that is easy to read, ideally 12pt and definitely not less than 10pt.

6. Leave some space between sections.

7. Leave spaces between slashes, e.g. three / four.

8. Ensure your CV is printed on good-quality white paper using a laser printer.

9. Don't fax your CV as the quality will not be good enough to scan.

10. Send your CV unfolded and unstapled, as either can cause misreading of the text.

11. Do not include anything that might confuse the software. This includes ampersands (&), hollow bullet points, currency symbols, unusual graphics and foreign characters.

12. Always spell check.

13. If emailing your CV, save it as a 'Text Only' document, and attach the text file to your email message/covering letter.

'There is so much advice out there on how to write a good CV, yet people still send employers CVs that are boring, messy and don't relate to the job. Then they wonder why they don't get shortlisted!'

Quote from an expert on CV writing

Useful web addresses for free CV-writing advice

www.bbc.co.uk/radio1/onelife/work/cvs/cvs_intro.shtml

www.scotcareers.co.uk and click on CV creator

www.alec.co.uk/cvtips/

www.businessballs.com/curriculum.htm

http://resume.monster.com

Chapter checklist

In this chapter we have looked at what needs to go into your CV. Some points to consider are:

- always give yourself plenty of time to prepare your CV
- gather all the information you need before you start
- present the information in your CV so that it is focused to the selection criteria
- blend in words from the selection criteria as you write
- use lots of positive words
- really sell your successes
- if no suitable job openings appear, consider sending your CV out 'on spec'.

Chapter five

CV layout options

You should read this chapter:

- when you have gathered together all the information you wish to include in a CV.

By the end of this chapter you should know:

- the variety of ways in which a CV can be presented

- the advantages and disadvantages of each format

- which format will best suit your purpose

- what steps to take if you decide to send out your CV speculatively ('on spec').

CV options

There is no single 'correct' way to present a CV, and this allows you to express your own creativity through your layout. However, there are certain conventions that should be followed. The exception to this would be if you are applying for a creative job, where a more adventurous approach might demonstrate your abilities.

Electronic CVs

Some employers advertise for staff on the web. And some of them are now adding CV templates so that you can send your CV directly by email. The advice given in this chapter will help you to make the most of whatever template you encounter.

Templates on your PC

Wordprocessing packages offer a variety of PC templates, and you might like to look at those before you start your CV to see if you think any of them will suit you. You should be able to complete any of them using the information in this chapter.

CV presentation tips

Do:

- make your information easy to read
- write a fresh version of your CV for each job – adapt it to match closely the criteria stated for the job
- get someone else to proof read your CV - it's difficult to spot your own mistakes.

Don't:

- use more than two sheets of A4 paper
- produce a double-sided CV
- use poor-quality paper
- use abbreviations, especially if they might be unfamiliar to the reader
- use only one CV for everything
- forget what you've written – use a copy of your CV as a crib sheet prior to interview

- assume that the reader will know what your past jobs involved
- forget which version of your CV you've sent – make a copy and note on it which job it relates to.

There are two main layout options for your CV:

1. the chronological CV
2. the skills based CV.

Chronological CV

As the name suggests, a chronological CV presents material in chronological (date) order. Information is usually presented in reverse order – that is, the most recent information is shown first. The chronological CV takes the reader step by step through your education history, then your work history and, finally, to your additional information.

'Sometimes candidates send in a CV with their application form. They write all over the application form 'see CV'. Why should I have to do all the work? I'm happy for them to send a CV, but they really must complete the application form as well. If they can't be bothered to do this, why should I be bothered to employ them?'

Quote from a company director

In graphical form, the chronological CV looks like this:

Name
Address
Telephone numbers
Email address

Professional profile

- write your statement here and mention some of your strengths as they relate to the criteria for the job

Key skills and competencies

- again, pick out key skills and competencies you possess in relation to the criteria

---

Education and training

- dates, names of schools
- details of exams

Career to date

- dates, name and address of employer
- job title
- responsibilities in that job
- any 'extras' you can claim

Additional information

- membership of clubs, awards, anything of interest that relates to the job in question

Interests

- show yourself to be a rounded person, make yourself seem positive and interesting

References

- name and contact details of two referees

Even within this format, there is a choice of how to present information. Remember, there are several ways to do this; choose whichever you prefer. The two golden rules are *make it easy for the reader to absorb the information you provide* and *ensure your information is relevant to the job*. This means presenting your information attractively and consistently, and in an order that relates to the selection criteria.

The advantage of the chronological CV is that it is the one most employers are familiar with, and they can find out a lot about you if they read this type of CV carefully. Chronological CVs also fill a single page, which is useful if you are young and don't yet have much experience to offer and therefore not much to write about.

This type of CV provides a useful reference guide for you when completing future CVs and, indeed, application forms. The only disadvantage is that it can be a fairly bland predictable read for a prospective interviewer. Make sure yours isn't!

But don't do this...

There is one 'wrong' way to write a CV and that is to mix styles. Look at this example:

Philipa Rudinsky,
123 Peterson Road,
Walmsley
Lancs
WM2 3ER
01333 568991 07878 654987
email philipa@robins.net

Education and training

Sept 2000–June 2005   Collett Community College, Warmsley

Qualifications:

GCSE

- English B
- Maths D
- textiles C
- business Studies A
- geography C

Qualifications:

Sept 2005–July 2006 Walmsley Regional College

- City and Guilds food preparation and cooking level 2
- Hazard Analysis Critical Control Point (HACCP)

Sept 2006–July 2007 Walmsley Regional College

Qualification:

- BTEC National Diploma in care

2.9.2006–present Walmsley Regional College

- OCR level 2 certificate text processing (part-time)

Career to date

Part-time work, while at school or college

NAS Newsagents, Victoria Lane, Walmsley

July 2002–February 2003

Saturday position involving handling money, dealing with customers, sorting out paper bills, and shelf filing.

Bakers Food Shops, Arthur Street, Walmsley 3.3.2003–3.9.2004

This job involved handling money, helping customers, filling shelves and working as part of a team.

Jane Pearce Elderly People's Home, Fortescue Road, Walmsley

Sept 2004–June 2007

I worked at Jane Pearce House in the kitchens as a weekend cook to support me through college. This involved the ability to supervise others, devise and cook menus as well as prepare the evening tea.

Full-time work since leaving college

Jane Pearce Elderly People's Home, Fortescue Road, Walmsley

July 2007–present

Care Assistant. This responsible role involved caring for elderly people, ambulance escort duty, collecting and banking money, and the supervision of others.

Other information

I enjoy working and being with others. I also enjoy swimming, needlepoint and dancing. I am a keen cook.

Can you spot the deliberate mistakes?

- no professional profile or competencies
- inconsistent use of commas at the end of lines in the address (tip – don't use any, it's not current business practice)
- inconsistent method of presenting dates, e.g. 3.9.2004 and Sept 2004 – make sure you use the same system throughout
- GCSEs – inconsistent use of capital letters
- spelling mistake – shelf 'filling' not 'filing'
- inconsistent use of underlining and bold to emphasise words
- not all the jobs show the job title, even though it is implied by the type of work undertaken – they should always be shown
- no referees.

Skills-based (or functional) CV

As the name suggests, this CV presentation is written to emphasise *skills* rather than take the reader chronologically through the life of the writer. This is an increasingly popular form of CV presentation, although it does require that you already have relevant skills or you'll find it difficult to fill a page! This type of CV is often used by people who are applying for jobs speculatively, or 'on spec' – that is, writing to employers who are not currently advertising a vacancy.

'People often emphasise their duties rather than their accomplishments. While employers want to know what they do in their job, they want to know what they've achieved even more. Try to show your successes.'

Quote from a recruitment specialist

To write a skills-based CV you simply do the same preparation as before, linking your skills with the job requirements. Then you present your skills in a punchy and eye-catching way. They are the main emphasis of this layout.

As you will see from the examples that follow, this type of CV does not state which skills have been used in which job. A skills-based CV often fits on one side of A4 paper.

Here are some examples of the format of this type of CV:

Name
Address
Telephone numbers
Email address

Professional profile

Education and training

- brief details only, showing key qualifications and courses

Capabilities

- list them here by using bullet points

Achievements

- again, list them here using bullet points – try to *quantify* your achievements

Career history

for each job list brief details of:

- employer's name and short address
- dates of employment
- job title

Additional information

- membership of relevant organisations, voluntary work, etc – unless you decide to provide this information in your covering letter

References

- name and contact details for two referees

Name

Address

Telephone numbers

Email

PROFESSIONAL PROFILE

- brief statement giving your key skills in relation to the job you are applying for

EDUCATION AND TRAINING

- brief details only, showing key qualifications and courses

KEY ACHIEVEMENTS

- list them here, relate them to the job and selection criteria

ONE SKILL AREA

- list skills under this heading using bullet points - relate them to selection criteria

ANOTHER SKILL AREA

- as before, list skills using bullet points - continue until you have shown all your relevant skills

CAREER HISTORY

For each job, list brief details of:

- employer's name and short address
- dates of employment
- job title

ADDITIONAL INFORMATION

(unless you decide to provide this information in your covering letter)

Collette's chronological CV

I'm assuming for this CV that Collette is looking for a secretarial job and is sending her CV out 'on spec' to a number of local companies. Note that she has stated at the top of the CV the type of work she is looking for. She would, of course, also mention this in her covering letter.

Collette Hay

27 Blinco Road

Wareham

Lancs LA5 8MM

collette.hay@plp.net

01333 787878 07879 64545

Job target: administrative or secretarial post

Professional profile and competencies

A conscientious and hardworking school-leaver with up-to-date secretarial skills. My particular strengths are:

- high level of accuracy
- typing at 45 wpm
- experience of Word: able to use 'Mail Merge', 'Tables' and 'Columns'
- PowerPoint: able to produce complex presentation material
- Excel: some experience of using formulae
- good team worker
- show initiative
- reliable

Key skills

- accurately typing letters and invoices
- filing efficiently
- excellent customer service skills
- reliable message taking
- accurate data entry
- skilful communicator

Career history

June 2007–Aug 2007

Hurst's Office Supplies Ltd, High Street, Wareham LA5 2NP

Administrative assistant – temporary post

- typing letters and invoices
- filing
- answering the telephone
- relief reception work

Whilst working at Hurst's I reorganised the filing system. As a result of this I achieved the 'Employee of the Month' Award.

Vacation work

July 2006–present

St Joseph's Home, Dear St, Wareham LA5 5NT

Day care assistant

- working with a variety of professionals
- dealing with a variety of personal needs of the residents
- writing diary notes on each resident
- dealing with the relatives of residents
- taking part in outings, etc.

Whilst working at St. Joseph's I invented a new board game for the residents, which has proved very popular.

Education and qualifications

2001–2007 St Joseph's Comprehensive, Wareham

GCSE

- English B
- mathematics A
- geography C
- history E
- art A
- business studies B
- OCR level 1 certificate in text processing

Additional information

For the past two years I have been secretary of the school drama club. This has given me a wide range of secretarial experience from taking minutes of meetings to handling monies from ticket sales. I enjoyed working as part of the team developing each drama production and also enjoyed working alone on those aspects of my secretarial role that required this. I am a keen photographer and also enjoy netball and swimming. I enjoy reading historical novels.

References

Mrs Jane Briggs, Manager
Hurst's Office Supplies
High Street
Wareham
Lancs LA5 2NP

Mr John Oman
7 Aubray Road
Wareham
Lancs LA5 4SN
(family friend)

How do you think Collette comes across? She is clearly a lively and enterprising person who enjoys being with others. She has a good range of exam passes relevant to the work she seeks. Additionally, she has managed to pass these whilst still taking on the work with the drama group and following her other hobbies. Most employers with a suitable vacancy would think she is a person worth seeing after reading this CV. Added to that, she has shown considerable initiative in sending it out 'on spec'.

Now we'll see how the CV looks in another format.

Collette's skills-based CV

Collette Hay
27 Blinco Road
Wareham
Lancs LA5 8MM

collette.hay@plp.net

01333 787878   07879 64545

Job target: administrative or secretarial post

PROFESSIONAL PROFILE AND COMPETENCIES

A conscientious and hardworking school-leaver with up-to-date secretarial skills. Key competencies include:

- accuracy
- typing at 45 wpm
- experience of Word, PowerPoint, Excel
- good team worker
- initiative
- reliability

KEY SKILLS

- accurately typing letters and invoices
- filing efficiently
- excellent customer service skills
- reliable message-taking
- accurate data entry

CAREER TO DATE

June 2007–Aug 2007

Hurst's Office Supplies Ltd, High Street, Wareham LA5 2NP

Administrative assistant – temporary post

July 2003–present

St Joseph's Home, Dear St, Wareham LA5 5NT

Day care assistant (vacation work)

QUALIFICATIONS

2007: 6 GCSEs – English B, mathematics A, geography C, history E, art A, business studies B

OCR level 1 certificate in text processing

ADDITIONAL INFORMATION

I am a conscientious and hard-working person who enjoys working as part of a team, but am also well motivated to work unsupervised. I pay good attention to detail and enjoy working to deadlines. I am a keen photographer and also enjoy netball and swimming. I am an enthusiastic reader of historical novels.

Put yourself in the shoes of the shortlister. She or he is looking for people who can meet those criteria outlined in the job description and person specification. The skills-based CV does save time checking skills, because they don't have to be hunted for in with a lot of other information. But, of course, the down side is that you can't present the same volume of information.

Spacing

As we've seen earlier, one rule on CV presentation is that you don't use more than two sides of A4 paper. As a school- or college/university-leaver you may find it difficult to fill two sides. Collette's skills-based CV, when presented on A4 paper, might fill only one side. In fact, this is very common for a skills-based CV. If it goes over to the second page she would have to make a decision either to space out the work so that it fills the second page, or to squash it up a bit to get it on one page.

Don't worry if the whole of page two isn't full, if necessary just send a one-page CV. If you decide to, you can 'squeeze' or 'expand' your information by:

- having bigger or smaller margins
- leaving more or less space between each heading
- listing examination results under or next to each other
- writing any addresses over one or more lines

- putting in, or leaving out, the words 'Curriculum vitae'
- putting the referees' names and addresses under or next to each other.

'The best tip I could give people writing CVs is to write a different version of their CV for each job. The information they give must match the requirements of the job.'

Quote from a CV writing expert

CV for a second job

James wants to apply for a job as trainee manager with a nationwide white goods store.

James's chronological CV

James Matthew Whiteways
27 High Meadows
Thornton
Derbyshire
DE13 1AH

01234 4455662   0889 656545

jamesm.whiteways23@nnt.com

PROFESSIONAL PROFILE AND COMPETENCIES

An enthusiastic and successful retail salesperson with outstanding experience of selling electrical equipment and stock control systems.

I can offer:

- keen customer awareness
- 100% reliability
- excellent record keeper
- flexible approach
- proven sales record
- good teamwork skills
- enthusiasm.

CAREER TO DATE

2006–present Hodder Electrical Ltd, Highgate Shopping Centre, Thornton

Salesperson

- specialist knowledge of all music systems, MP3s, PDAs, video/DVD recorders and cameras
- responsibility for stock control when manager is away

During the past year at Hodder Electrical Ltd I have increased sales in my department by 15%.

2005–2006 Campbell's Shoes Ltd, Twenty Street, Thornton

Salesperson (Saturdays and vacation)

- shoe sales
- measuring children's feet
- cash handling
- credit card handling
- stockroom work

During my time at Campbell's the manager received six compliments about my work from customers.

2003–2005 The Corner Shop, 23 Garden Road, Thornton

Newspaper delivery

- accurate newspaper delivery
- money collection

EDUCATION AND QUALIFICATIONS

2001–2006 Wells Community College, Thornton

GCSE

- English B
- maths C
- art C
- history E
- geography D
- French E

TRAINING

2006   Staff induction: two-week course

2007   Effective Selling Skills: three-day, in-house course

INTERESTS

I am an enthusiastic footballer and a member of Thornton Sports and Social Club Committee, where I have responsibility for social activities. I enjoy reading thrillers and socialising with friends.

ADDITIONAL INFORMATION

- clean driving licence
- excellent health

REFERENCES

Mrs J Whitemore
Branch manager
Hodder Electrical Ltd
Highgate Shopping Centre
Thornton DE12 4EE
01234 556889
jkw@hodderelectrical.net

Mr B Michaels
Branch manager
Campbell's Shoes Ltd
Twenty Street
Thornton DE12 5RL
01234 52324
info@campbellshoes.com

James's skills-based CV

James Matthew Whiteways
27 High Meadows, Thornton, Derbyshire DE13 1HL
01234 4455662 0889 656545
jamesm.whiteways23@nnt.com

PROFESSIONAL PROFILE

An enthusiastic and successful retail salesperson with outstanding experience of selling electrical equipment and stock control.

I can offer:

- keen customer awareness
- 100% reliability
- excellent record keeping
- flexible approach
- proven sales record
- good teamwork skills
- enthusiasm.

KEY SKILLS AND COMPETENCIES

- knowledge of white goods of all sorts
- specialist knowledge of videos, DVDs, MP3s, DPAs, music systems and cameras
- managing stock-control systems
- working to targets
- working knowledge of wordprocessing
- excellent customer service

ACCOMPLISHMENTS

Increased sales in video and music systems department by 15% in one year. I was 'Employee of the Month' three months running this year.

CAREER HISTORY

2006–present   Salesperson

Hodder Electrical Ltd, Highgate Shopping Centre, Thornton

2005–2006   Salesperson (part time, weekends and vacations)

Campbell's Shoes Ltd, Twenty Street, Thornton

2002–2004   Newspaper delivery

The Corner Shop, 23 Garden Road, Thornton

EDUCATION AND TRAINING

Effective Sales Skills – three-day, in-house course

6 GCSEs including English (B) and maths (C)

ADDITIONAL INFORMATION

I am a highly motivated and successful salesperson who enjoys working as part of a team. I am presentable and relate well to customers. I find that staff often turn to me for advice on a variety of matters. I am an enthusiastic footballer and a member of Thornton Sports and Social Club Committee, where I have responsibility for social activities. I enjoy reading thrillers and socialising with friends.

'A good CV can be spoilt by candidates writing a shoddy covering letter. Both should be written with absolute professionalism.'

Quote from an editor in a publishing company

CV for graduates with some work experience

Sally is a graduate with work experience. She is applying for a job as a researcher with a pressure group working for reform of the prison system. Both her chronological and skills-based CV follow. Spend a few minutes comparing the two. Consider jobs you might apply for and decide which CV would suit your needs best.

Sally Jane Dowling's chronological CV:

Sally Jane Dowling
27 Upper North Street
Dainow DN23 6PB
01229 868686   07876 345632
sallyjane.dowling@ttl.net

PROFESSIONAL PROFILE

An energetic and enthusiastic researcher with experience of working in penal reform. My experience and education mean that I can offer the following skills and knowledge:

- excellent attention to detail
- qualitative and quantitative research experience
- knowledge of the criminal justice system
- competent user of all Microsoft Office products

Key competencies

- excellent project planning skills
- respect for diversity
- ability to prioritise both long- and short-term work
- skilled at multidisciplinary working
- innovative
- work within budget
- meet deadlines

CAREER TO DATE

2002–2004 North East London Probation Service

High Tower, East Street, Stratford, SF12 3WE

Probation assistant

In this busy post I was responsible for:

- interviewing probationers
- writing reports
- co-leading groups
- liaising with other professionals
- attending case conferences.

2001–2001 Dainow Coffee Company

22 High Street, Dainow DN23 2SF

Saturday sales assistant

- serving customers
- answering the telephone
- money handling

EDUCATION AND QUALIFICATIONS

2004–2007 University of North London

BA (Hons) social research 2.1

1995–2002 Dainow Comprehensive College

GCE A level: sociology A, English B, history D

GCSEs: English, mathematics, history, sociology, geography, religious studies, art

VOLUNTARY WORK

2003–2004 Volunteer teacher on Rightstart literacy course at Dainow Prison.

2006–2007 Member of The Howard League Penal Reform Group.

ADDITIONAL INFORMATION

I have a long-term interest in the field of criminology and penal reform. My dissertation at university was on 'Problems faced by prisoners' families' and won the Jane McDonald Award for best dissertation of the year. I very much enjoyed the research element of my degree, which lasted two years, and I feel enthusiastic about pursuing penal reform as a career.

I am a friendly, outgoing person and have a passion for computing. I enjoy working as part of a team, but am well motivated to work on my own.

LEISURE INTERESTS

I am a bit of a film buff and enjoy old movies as well as current releases. I belong to a squash club where I play regularly. I love reading, especially family novels and suspense thrillers.

REFEREES

Amanda O'Connor, Team manager
North East London Probation Service
High Tower
East Street
Stratford SF12 3WE
0207 565 444
a.oconnor@nelp.org.uk

Richard Digby, Governor
Dainow Prison
Long Road
Dainow DN9 8PO
01229 876543
r.digby@dainowprison.org

... and now a skills-based version:

Sally Jane Dowling
27 Upper North Street
Dainow DN23 6PB
01229 868686   0889 656545
sallyjane.dowling@ttl.net

Professional profile

An energetic and enthusiastic researcher with experience of working in penal reform. My experience and education mean that I can offer the following skills and knowledge:

- excellent attention to detail
- qualitative and quantitative research experience
- knowledge of the criminal justice system
- competent user of all Microsoft Office products.

Key competencies

- excellent project planning skills
- respect for diversity

- skilled at multidisciplinary working
- innovative
- work within budget
- meet deadlines

Relevant research experience

'Problems faced by prisoners' families'; qualitative research.
Evaluation of effectiveness of groups in probation.
Two-year study of research methods in BA.

Key skills

Writing

- writing up research findings
- writing reports
- writing diary records, and group and case work

Communicating

- multi-agency working
- attending case conferences
- dealing with a variety of clients
- working as part of a probation team
- interviewing prisoners' families

Computing

- MS Office
- SSAS research package
- Publisher

Employment

2002–2004 North East London Probation Service, **Probation assistant**
2001–2001 Dainow Coffee Company, **Saturday sales assistant**

Achievements

I won the Jane McDonald Award at university for best dissertation in my year. This was on 'Problems faced by prisoners' families.'

Education and qualifications

2007 BA (hons) social research 2.1, University of North London

Additional information

I have a long-term interest in the field of criminology and penal reform. My dissertation at university was on 'Problems faced by prisoners' families' and won the Jane McDonald Award for best dissertation of the year. I very much enjoyed the research element of my degree, which lasted two years, and I feel enthusiastic about pursuing penal reform as a career. I am a friendly, outgoing person and have a passion for computing. I enjoy working as part of a team, but am well motivated to work on my own.

Leisure interests

I am a bit of a film buff and enjoy old movies as well as current releases. I belong to squash club where I play regularly. I love reading, especially family novels and suspense thrillers.

References

Amanda O'Connor, Team manager
North East London Probation Service
High Tower
East Street
Stratford SF12 3WE
0207 565 444
a.oconnor@nelp.org.uk

Richard Digby, Governor
Dainow Prison
Long Road
Dainow DN9 8PO
01229 876543
r.digby@dainowprison.org

In the skills-based version Sally may have chosen to leave out the 'Additional information' and to include it in her covering letter instead. The fact that Sally had won an award for an outstanding dissertation as an undergraduate would be of great interest to a prospective employer. It is well worth, therefore, including it under a heading of 'Achievements'. If you choose a skills-based format for your CV this could be where you provide information on those things you have done that are over and above what is normally expected at work or college.

'There is no second chance to make a good first impression. Get your CV right first time.'

Quote from the manager of a CV writing company

Practical considerations

Here are some points to remember to ensure your CV looks attractive:

- don't make your CV look cramped: leave plenty of 'white space' around your words

- leave a good margin around your text, about 25 mm

- use single spacing generally, but double spacing between paragraphs

- be consistent in the way you present information – make reading as easy as possible

- use good quality paper – 80 gsm at least

- always keep in mind – *'does this look like a document I would want to read?'.*

By the way, always keep some spare paper so that you can write your covering letter on the same stuff.

Chapter checklist

- Be consistent in the way you present material – make it easy for the reader to shortlist you.

- Decide which CV style would best present the information you want to show.

- Make yourself come alive as a person, rather than just a list of facts.

Chapter six

More sample CVs

You should read this chapter:

- when you need to prepare a CV for either a specific job or for a general mailing to a number of organisations.

By the end of this chapter you should:

- have a much clearer idea of what a range of CVs look like
- be able to select the CV for your needs.

A reminder

Do remember that the following CVs are just examples of the types of layout you might like to consider. Your own layout is up to you. Do, however, read the previous chapters to help you to make the best possible decision.

'If your CV is visually too busy, with lots of different fonts and colours, you'll give the shortlister a headache and they won't be well disposed towards you.'

Quote from a recruitment adviser

Sample CVs

Example CV for a further education college leaver – 1

Jane Collinson
22 Corfield Road
Swansea SA3 7RG
01792 554467   0879 654321
jane.collinson@ntn.net

PROFESSIONAL PROFILE

Recent college leaver with excellent administrative and wordprocessing skills. I am a quick learner, flexible and enjoy working as part of a team. I can offer the following competencies:

- good attention to detail
- using initiative
- ability to maintain confidentiality
- ability to meet deadlines
- pride in my work
- pursue goals with confidence
- seek ways to improve performance.

KEY SKILLS

- excellent written and verbal communication skills
- typing at 35 wpm
- some knowledge of Excel
- skilled at producing PowerPoint slides
- accurate at filing

EMPLOYMENT HISTORY

Feb 2007 **Harper Building Society**, High Street, Llandor, Swansea SA9 3LK
During my two weeks' work experience with this building society I was involved in:

- opening and distributing the post
- filing
- operating the switchboard
- sending information out to customers
- typing.

Jan–Nov 2006   **Rebecca's Greengrocery**, 247 Maldon Road, Swansea SA1 3PS

Saturday assistant Whilst working at Rebecca's my tasks included:

- unloading produce vans
- arranging produce attractively
- checking quality of produce
- serving customers
- handling cash.

EDUCATION AND QUALIFICATIONS

2006–2007   Llandor Regional College, Pailthorpe Road, Llandor SA13 4RP

BTEC Word Intermediate Award in ICT
GCE A level English
NVQ 2 customer service

2001–2006   Llandor Comprehensive School, Swanns Road, Llandor SA4 9OL

GCSEs

- English language
- English literature
- textile and design
- maths
- geography
- history
- German

INTERESTS AND HOBBIES

I have many interests. I enjoy reading historical novels, doing embroidery, socialising with friends and swimming. I also attend an exercise class twice a week.

ADDITIONAL INFORMATION

For the past six months I have been helping run our local Brownie pack, and this has given me valuable experience not just in working with children, but also in record keeping, financial management (which Brown Owl has delegated to me) and dealing with a range of unexpected and sometimes difficult situations.

REFERENCES

Mr T Thomas
Harper Building Society
High Street
Llandor
Swansea SA9 3LK
01729 883210

Katherine Calvin
Llandor Comprehensive School
Swanns Road
Llandor
Swansea SA7 6CV
01729 453234
k.calvin@calvin.web

> 'Several times I have found that people have given out-of-date mobile numbers on their CV. I go to phone them to invite them to interview and can't get through. It immediately makes them look sloppy.'
>
> Quote from a manager of a retail store

Example CV for a further education college leaver – 2

JONATHON EDMUNDS
33 Snetterton Road
Wellesbourne SA33 5RA
01889 545470   07879 654098
email: j.edmunds@global.net

PERSONAL PROFILE

I am sociable, lively and have good communication skills. I get on well with most people, am renowned for keeping cool under pressure, and enjoy learning new skills.

KEY SKILLS AND COMPETENCIES

- attention to detail
- creative problem solving
- excellent customer service skills
- loyalty
- conscientious approach
- team player
- able to use own initiative
- good time management

EDUCATION AND QUALIFICATIONS

2005–2007   Wellesbourne Community College, Wellesbourne SA33 3RR
NVQ level 3 in business studies

2000–2005   Wellesbourne Comprehensive School, Baker Street,
Wellesbourne SA33 4WW

GCSEs:

English A	social studies B
maths A	child development C
history B	media studies C

TRAINING

2005   First Aid Certificate, St John Ambulance, Stratford-upon-Avon, Warwickshire.
2006   Food Hygiene Basic, Chefcall, London SW1 1EE.

WORK EXPERIENCE

2004–present   Speedy Pizza, High Street, Wellesbourne SA33 5TY

Waiter - Evening and weekend work at this busy pizza restaurant and take-away.

My duties include:

- waiting at tables
- money handling
- answering the phone and taking orders
- working as part of a team.

April–May 2004   Rototech Ltd, Bullon Business Park, The Fairway, Wellesbourne

Office assistant – Work experience. My duties included:

- photocopying
- dealing with incoming and outgoing post
- entering data on database
- filing.

ACHIEVEMENTS

In school – active member of Wellesbourne Community College Student Union.

In college – made scenery for school plays two years running.

INTERESTS AND HOBBIES

I enjoy sport and play in the college's football team. I enjoy popular music and going to the cinema with friends.

ADDITIONAL INFORMATION

Full clean driving licence

Health: excellent

REFERENCES

Ms Jean Willers, Principal
Wellesbourne Community College
Burns Road
Wellesbourne SA33 3RR
01294 299384

Dawn Collins, Manager
Speedy Pizza
High Street
Wellesbourne SA33 5TY
01294 494837

'I once received a CV that was 14 pages long. I couldn't be bothered to read it. It went straight in the bin'.

Quote from a manager in the NHS

Example CV for a further education college leaver – 3 (skills-based)

MAYA SINGH
16 Wilberforce Road
Manchester M14 6BD
0980 545489
Nationality: British

SKILLS PROFILE

- awareness of health and safety requirements
- advise and consult with clients
- shampoo and condition hair and scalp
- cut hair using basic techniques
- style, dress and finish hair using basic techniques
- change hair colour using basic techniques
- perm, relax and neutralise hair
- perm, relax and neutralise African Caribbean hair
- fulfil salon reception duties
- bilingual English/Bengali

PERSONAL QUALITIES AND COMPETENCIES

- self starter
- reliable
- always meet deadlines
- language proficiency
- English and Bengali fluent
- French and German to GCSE standard

EMPLOYMENT HISTORY

Nov 2006–present **Looking Good Hairdressers**, Alma Road, Manchester M13 5TT

Saturday hairdressing assistant
Reception duties including answering telephone, filing and greeting customers. Assisting hairdressing, including shampooing hair, applying hair colorant under supervision. Cutting and styling hair under supervision on model nights.

Dec 2005–Nov 2006 **The Corner Shop**, Wilberforce Road, Salford, Manchester M14 6BD

Newspaper delivery person
Paper round, delivering papers correctly. Money collection.

EDUCATION AND QUALIFICATIONS

Sept 2005–Jun 2007 Manchester Regional College, Elm Street, Manchester
M14 8RW
NVQ 2 hairdressing

2000–2005 Maple Community College, Maple Road, Manchester M14 3DE

GCSEs: maths (E), geography (B), religious studies (D), English (B).

INTERESTS

I am a member of the college girl's football team. I also enjoy reading, cooking and learning languages.

REFERENCES

Mrs Jason, Manager
Looking Good Hairdressers
Alma Road
Manchester M13 5TT
0161 456789

Timothy Snell, Tutor
Manchester Regional College
Elm Street
Manchester M14 8RW
0161 654321
tim.snell@manregcoll.com

'The biggest howler I've seen on a CV was when someone said: 'I received a Plague for Consultant of the Year'. It gave us all a good laugh, but also told us this person didn't bother to proofread.'

Quote from a manager in a local authority

Example CV for a graduate writing speculatively – 1

Jane Blanton
35 Birmingham Road
Solihull
BM1 3LL
0121 330 4455 07978 456234
jane.blanton@talknet.com

CAREER OBJECTIVE – Management Traineeship

Professional Profile and Competencies

A self-motivated, hardworking **business studies graduate** with work experience in retail.

Good customer service skills and keen to develop further abilities. I can offer the ability to:

- lead individuals and teams
- set standards
- consult effectively
- work towards corporate goals
- communicate effectively
- understand and work to policies
- speak fluent French.

EDUCATION AND QUALIFICATIONS

2004–2007	Warwick University, **business studies, BA (honours) 2.1**
2002–2004	Marlow Sixth Form College, Hills Road, West Wickham, CB3 3RR GCE A levels: business studies A, English language A, English literature B, media studies B.
1997–2002	Marlow Comprehensive School, Plough Street, West Wickham CB4 4RR GCSEs: English, maths, science, geography, design and technology, religious studies, French

TRAINING

| Dec 2002 | McGregors Customer Service Training, McGregors Hygiene Training |

CAREER TO DATE

| Oct 2005 –present | Neve's Ltd, The High Street, Warwick, CV2 4RG **Sales associate.** Ladies fashion store – weekends and vacations |

For the past six months I have successfully acted as manager when the manager and deputy manager are not present. This involves:

- dealing with day-to-day management decisions relating to the running of the store
- ensuring that customer satisfaction is high at all times.

When both managers are present, I am part of the sales team, involving:

- serving customers
- ensuring stock levels are correct
- working as part of a team
- cash handling
- working in changing rooms.

Dec 2004   McGregors, Greens Road, West Wickham CB4 8FA.
–July 2005 **Sales assistant.**

My part-time post with McGregors has given me experience of:

- working as part of a team
- working in a high-pressure fast-food environment
- ensuring that my work was hygienic at all times
- customer service
- cash handling.

ACHIEVEMENTS

- member of university netball team
- member of French conversation group

INTERESTS AND HOBBIES

My family and I go camping in France most summers and I speak French fluently. I enjoy spending time with friends, going to the cinema and dancing. I like to read, mostly romance and crime stories.

ADDITIONAL INFORMATION

- Full, clean driving licence
- Excellent health

REFERENCES

Mrs G. Jones, Manager   Mrs McGregor
Neve's Fashions   McGregors
The High Street   Greens Road
Warwick CV2 4RG   West Wickham CB4 8FA
01987 565789   01987 343212
genie@nevefashions.com

'Now that there is legislation against ageism at work, it is not necessary to put your date of birth on your CV.'

Quote from a recruitment specialist

Example CV for a graduate writing speculatively – 2

James Robinson
231 Upper High Street
Cambridge CB4 5LF
01223 554633 0876 676908
james@robinson.com

TARGET VACANCY – SOCIAL SCIENCE RESEARCHER

PROFESSIONAL PROFILE

A hardworking graduate with keen interest in, and commitment to, social issues. My interests have given me invaluable experience in the field of research and dealing with difficult people and situations.

QUALIFICATIONS

Anglia Ruskin University, East Road, Cambridge CB1 2ER

2004–2007   BA social sciences 2.1

My course included economics, politics, sociology, philosophy, geography and statistics.

2002–2004   Hills Road Sixth Form College, Cambridge

GCE A levels: English (B), sociology (A), psychology (A), history (B)

OUTSTANDING ACHIEVEMENT

My thesis was on deprivation within inner cities in Britain. I was awarded the Williams Prize for best thesis of the year.

KEY SKILLS

I can offer excellent experience in:

- **qualitative and quantitative** research methods
- use of **Excel**
- succinct and accurate **report writing**
- collaborative **team work**
- **project management**.

CAREER TO DATE

April 2007–present   **Bath Inner City Survey**, Grosvenor Road, Bath BA2 1ET

Researcher – this temporary post has given me good experience of:

- qualitative research methods
- methodical working
- business environment
- working as part of a team.

Sept 2003–Apr 2007 **B and Y DIY Store**, Huntingdon Road, Cambridge CB4 3BN
Weekend clerical assistant
This part-time post offered me considerable experience in:

- office routine

- handling difficult situations

- customer service.

INTERESTS

I am keen on keeping fit and as well as playing several sports. I attend a circuit class once a week. I also enjoy travel and spending time with friends.

ADDITIONAL INFORMATION

I have a full clean driving licence. I was involved with stage design for a local amateur dramatics society for two years whilst at college. I have good keyboard skills and can design a simple web page.

REFERENCES

Mr T Edwards	Ms K Lee
Bath Inner City Survey	27 Declan Street
Grosvenor Road	Cambridge
Bath BA2 1ET	CB3 2QW
01876 839281	01223 434909
tony.edwards@bics.com	

'I don't even bother to look at CVs that don't have a covering letter attached.'

Quote from a manager in an IT company

Chapter seven

Job and Apprenticeship application forms

You should read this chapter:

- before you begin to complete a job or Apprenticeship application form.

By the end of this chapter you should know how to:

- use your self-analysis
- present information about yourself
- use job descriptions, person specifications and competencies (selection criteria) to help you decide what to write
- use evidence of success.

Application forms

Application forms are easy! Read this chapter and you'll realise they are a doddle ...

There are several advantages to completing application forms. The format is prepared for you; you simply have to fill in the spaces and sometimes the space provided suggests how much you should write.

The form also tells you what information to provide, as well as the format, and this saves you having to make decisions about these issues.

One disadvantage is that you may have little flexibility to express yourself. Also, it is difficult to complete an application form using a wordprocessor. However, many organisations have their forms on the web and you can often send them electronically; even if you can't, you can often fill in the application form on your computer, print it off and then post it. Some organisations use the same form for applicants for all of their jobs, and so it may be difficult to find a space to provide the specific information you want to get across.

Section: 'Biographical information'

All application forms ask you for similar information: name, address, date of birth, career history, etc.

To complete this section successfully:

- read the instructions carefully and follow them exactly

- practise on a spare copy, if necessary (forms full of crossings out and spelling mistakes, or errors such as putting today's date as your date of birth do not impress an employer)

- write legibly, using black ink if asked to do so

- be consistent in the way you present information

- take care with abbreviations, jargon, etc – only use them if you are sure the shortlister will understand them

- check everything twice, preferably asking someone else to read it through as well (we tend to see what we expect to see, rather than what is actually there).

When it comes to stating your 'Reasons for leaving' a previous job you may need to use tact. There are a few golden rules about explaining why you left a job. Here they are:

- always try to make the reason for leaving sound positive rather than negative – e.g. something you wanted to go to, rather than something you wanted to get away from

- try to avoid saying you were sacked if you can, but don't tell a lie

- don't say something like, *'Because I didn't get on with the boss'* – the reader will not know this person and may wonder if you are a trouble-maker

- employers like to see that people have moved on for logical reasons – for promotion, to widen skills and experience, because of relocation from one part of the country to another, to return to education, etc

- mentioning redundancy can be OK, although sometimes employers may wonder why you were chosen to be made redundant – if this was because the company or department was closed down then say so, rather than simply saying *'made redundant'*.

For qualifications, present your information in a consistent and easy-to-read manner. This means not mixing, for example, 3 August 2007 with 3.8.07. If any of your qualifications are unusual or were obtained abroad you may want to add an explanatory note so that the shortlister can make comparisons with other qualifications.

Declaration

Simply your signature and the date. If you send in your form electronically, you will be asked to sign it when you attend for interview. Remember that all application forms should be accompanied by a covering letter, however brief. Look at Chapter nine for further details if you need advice on this.

Equal opportunities forms

Some application forms also have an 'Equal opportunities' section. Often this is a separate sheet or one that is torn off the main application form. Organisations use this information to check whether they are discriminating against any groups. In many organisations this information is detached from the form before the shortlister sees it.

Section: 'Give information in support of your application'

Almost all forms have the 'Give information in support of your application' box – usually the biggest box. Luckily, this page is dead easy to complete when you know the trick.

But let's go back a step. If you have read the previous chapters you will already have collected a mass of relevant information about yourself, which you can use in this section. If you have not read these chapters yet, do go back and do so. They include a range of activities to help you to analyse yourself and your skills, and to work out the best way to sell yourself.

For each job you are interested in, you will need to go through this process again, albeit in less detail. Your aim will be to match what you say about yourself to the selection criteria supplied to you, as well as to anything you know about the organisation. Remember, even if you are not supplied with these documents, you can make a fair job of working out what they would be by doing some research.

Let me recap on some of the major points:

- you need to identify your skills and experience relevant to the job you are applying for
- you should be able to write about yourself using a range of 'positive' words
- you should have identified those things about yourself that make you stand out from the crowd
- you should be able to write about the competencies that prove you are the person for the job (see Chapter two to remind yourself how to do this).

As you plan how to complete this section, keep these points in mind and try to get inside the reader's head. Try to work out what they are looking for and how you can show that you have it (or at least some of it); refer back to Chapter three if you need to. With this preparation in mind you are almost ready to start on the form.

'People can fail to get an interview because of poorly completed application forms. Our company sends with the form details of how to complete it. Amazingly, a lot of people ignore that advice. This does not show attention to detail or even common sense.'

Quote from a manager of an accountancy firm

To complete this section of the form, follow these simple steps.

1. Check if the form, or guidance notes on how to complete it if provided, tells you what the selection criteria are. They are almost always the job description, person specification, competencies or a combination of any of these.

2. At the top of this section write a general introduction. Something like *'In support of my application I will provide examples of my experience in the same order as shown in the selection criteria'.* Before that, you could also include the professional profile as described in Chapter four.

3. For each of the criteria write something about your experience of that item. Use the STAR method you read about in Chapter two. *This is absolutely vital – your shortlisters will be judging you against your responses to their stated criteria.*

You can number your paragraphs in the same way as the criteria. But even if you don't number them, you should write about them in the order in which they are shown. There are some examples in Chapter two. Here a couple more.

Examples

'Describe how your groupwork skills resulted in the successful achievement of a task.'

STAR answer:

'During the final year of my psychology degree, I led a team to investigate the response of individuals to potentially dangerous situations. I called a meeting of the team to plan a strategy for action. I then delegated tasks to each individual. I gave them clear goals and deadlines and established how each would be monitored. As a result, our project was not only on time but gained the highest marks out of all the teams for our year.'

'Describe a time when you had to work under stress.'

STAR answer:

'In the second year of my degree I had two major assignments that had to be handed in within a two-week period. I let the time slip away from me with other distractions until I had too little time left. I had to cancel all social engagements and work non-stop. At the last minute my printer broke down and I had to ask a friend to print off my work. I did get the work in on time but it was stressful. From that experience I learned to be

more organised, break big tasks into smaller steps, each with their own deadline, and to allow time for things to go wrong.'

(Whilst you are writing about something you did wrong here, you are showing that you have been reflective and have learned from the experience.)

It may be that the criteria are not written out as a question but as a list. The two examples above could simply be written as:

- groupwork skills

- working under stress.

No matter, simply write about them in the same way, using the STAR approach.

Easy!

So few candidates understand how to do this that you'll be streets ahead if you follow these simple steps.

Many organisations use a generic application form, such as the one shown here.

Application form	Date:
Vacancy:	Manager:
Candidate name:	Address:
Telephone:	Email:
Nationality:	Do you need a work permit for permanent employment in the UK? Yes/No Do you have one? Yes/No
Do you have a driving licence? Yes/No	

Education and qualifications			
Please list all qualifications held or currently studied for. List the most recent first. State grades achieved.			
Dates	**School/university**	**Qualification**	**Results**

Employment history

Please briefly describe any work that you have undertaken (paid or voluntary). Please write about the most recent first.

From To Month/year		Employer	Job title/ responsibilities	Achievements

Personal interests and achievements

Please list below any relevant part-time activities. Provide dates and year. Include any activities that require skills and abilities relevant to our selection criteria.

Why you are applying for this post?

Explain why you are applying for this particular post. Provide details of any relevant skills or training not already provided.

Additional information

Write here any additional information that will support your application.

Referees

Please give the names and contact details of two referees.

Name:	Name:
Position:	Position:
Address:	Address:
Telephone:	Telephone:
Email:	Email:

Availability

Please give dates when you are **not** available for interview.	Please give the date from which you are available for employment.

Declaration

I sign here to state that the information provided in this form is true. I understand that false statements may jeopardise my application. This can lead to offers of employment being withdrawn.

Signed .... Name (print) .... Date ....

To show you how to complete a form what follows is a real application form from Cambridgeshire County Council, followed by the council's guidlines for completion.

Although advice is focused on this form, the points given in this chapter would apply to other forms you may have to complete.

Cambridgeshire County Council

Confidential

Making equality a reality

A P P L I C A T I O N   F O R M

Please read the guidance notes before completing this form.

JOB DETAILS

Application for	

Directorate		**Reference No.**	

PERSONAL DETAILS

Surname		**Initials**	

Address for correspondence	

Tel. No. (Home)		**Mobile/Work Tel No**	

EDUCATION (from age 11)

School/College/University attended	Certificates/Qualifications obtained	Dates from and to (month/year)

Membership of professional bodies or other relevant qualifications

Details of relevant training courses	month/year

PRESENT OR MOST RECENT EMPLOYMENT (including unpaid activities)

Name of Employer

Address

Post Held

month/year

Date started

Notice required if applicable

Current Salary

Present Employment ☐   **Recent Employment** ☐   (Please Indicate)

Main Duties and Responsibilities

PREVIOUS EMPLOYMENT (continue on a separate sheet if necessary)

Have you previously worked for Cambridgeshire County Council? Yes ☐ No ☐

If yes, please include below with details of all previous employment:

Employer's name and address	Post held	Dates from & to Month/Year	Reason for Leaving

HOW YOU MEET THE SELECTION CRITERIA
(read guidance notes before completing)

REFEREES

Name		Name	

Address Including E-mail

Address Including E-mail

Tel. No.

Tel. No.

Occupation or Relationship to you

Occupation or Relationship to you

May we contact your referee prior to interview if shortlisted? Yes [ ] No [ ]

Yes [ ] No [ ]

REHABILITATION OF OFFENDERS ACT

Have you been convicted, cautioned or court martialled for any relevant criminal offence? Yes [ ] No [ ]

Is there any relevant court action pending against you? Yes [ ] No [ ]

DECLARATION

I confirm that the information I have given on this form is correct and complete and that misleading statements may be sufficient for cancelling any agreements made. I understand that, in the event of being shortlisted for interview, I will be required to complete a confidential declaration in respect of my health. *Because of the sensitive nature of the duties that the postholder may sometimes be expected to undertake, I also understand that a "Declaration of Criminal Record" form may have to be completed.* This will include details of any criminal convictions, cautions, reprimands and final warnings and any other information that may have a bearing on my suitability for the post *whether spent or not.*
*The part in italics only applies to posts requiring a Standard or Enhanced Level of Disclosure.

Are you related to, or do you have a close personal relationship with, any Councillor or employee of Cambridgeshire County Council.

Yes [ ] No [ ]

If yes, please state their name and position

I declare that all the above information is correct.

Signature

Date

Return the completed form to: Recruitment Team, Cambridgeshire County Council, Box ELH 1403,Shire Hall, Castle Hill, Cambridge, CB3 0AP.
E-mail to recruitment@cambridgeshire.gov.uk

Confidential

MONITORING FORM

Reference no: [   ]

E-Mail Address: [   ]

First Names: [   ]

	Mr	Ms	Miss	Mrs
Title:	☐	☐	☐	☐

Other [   ]

	Male	Female
Gender:	☐	☐

	Day	Month	Year
Date of birth			

Ethnic Origin:

Asian or Asian British – Bangladeshi	☐
Asian or Asian British – Indian	☐
Asian or Asian British – Pakistani	☐
Any other Asian background	☐
Black or Black British – African	☐
Black or Black British – Caribbean	☐
Any other Black background	☐
Chinese	☐
White – British	☐
White – Irish	☐
White – Other	☐
Any other ethnic group	☐
Mixed – white and Asian	☐
Mixed – White and Black African	☐
Mixed – White and Black Caribbean	☐
Any other mixed background	☐
Not specified	☐

Do you have a disability?

Yes [   ]   No [   ]

Where did you see this post advertised?

[   ]

When?	Day	Month	Year

Do you require a work permit ?

Yes [   ]   No [   ]

National Insurance No./Work permit details

[   ]

CAMBRIDGESHIRE COUNTY COUNCIL

EQUAL OPPORTUNITIES

Equity is one of the Council's five core values. The Council is committed to equality of opportunity both in service delivery and people management.

To help us monitor the reality of our equality policies, please complete the applicant monitoring form.

We cannot monitor the success or otherwise of our policies without it.

Thank you.

Chief Executive

Guidelines for completion of the Application Form

The application form, as opposed to a curriculum vitae (CV), is used to ensure that information is presented in a standardised format and that only the details that we require are provided. This ensures that all applicants are treated fairly and equally.

As the information contained on the form is used during the selection process, it is essential that you complete all sections as fully as possible. If there is not enough space provided on the form, please continue on a separate sheet of paper, do not attach a CV. On each sheet used, write your name, reference number and the post applied for, together with the section you are answering.

- Please complete the form using black ink.
- If any section does not apply to you, please write N/A.

The following notes are intended to assist you with the completion of the application form.

Personal Details

- Please do not provide your first name. Only your initials are needed to ensure that all applicants are considered fairly whether they are male or female. We request that you tell us your first name on the Monitoring Form.

Education (from age 11)

- School/College/University attended

Give details of secondary and any further education received, including dates and qualification(s) attained.

- Membership of professional bodies or other relevant qualifications

Provide details of the professional bodies to which you belong and any professional qualification(s) relevant to your application.

- Details of relevant training courses

Include the details of any relevant short courses or evening classes attended, including dates.

Present Employment

This section requests the details of your current employment or most recent employment, including voluntary activities. You should:

- Provide a brief description of the duties and responsibilities held during this employment.
- Include any duties that you consider to be of particular relevance to the position for which you are applying.
- Provide details of those jobs (paid or unpaid) that you intend to continue – the Working Time Regulations require the Council to monitor the hours that you work each week, including hours worked in other organisations.

- Indicate whether the employment is present or recent in the box provided.
- Provide your current salary or pay per hour.
- Indicate if you have been previously employed with Cambridgeshire County Council and provide the appropriate detail

Previous Employment

- Provide details of all previous employment, including that of a voluntary nature. The information should be provided in date order, starting with the most recent.
- Do not include your current employment in this section.

How You meet the Selection Criteria

Use this section to provide any other useful information about yourself and how you meet the essential criteria of the person specification, e.g:

- How do your abilities and experience make you suitable for the post?
- Why are you applying for the post?
- If the job requires mobility, can you drive, do you have a clean licence and do you have use of a car or other motor vehicle?
- What are your interests outside of work?

Referees

- Please provide the details of TWO people who may be approached for a reference.
- If you are employed, one referee must be connected with your current employment, i.e. your manager or supervisor.
- If you are a school or college leaver, please give details of a teacher or tutor.
- A suitable second referee would be a previous employer, business associate or leader/organiser of a voluntary organisation.
- Family members, friends or people with whom you have any other significant relationship are not acceptable referees.
- Please indicate whether you are happy for us to contact your referees if you are shortlisted for interview.

Rehabilitation of Offenders Act

You should complete this section if:

- you have been cautioned, court martialled or have criminal convictions that are not considered 'spent' under the Rehabilitation of Offenders Act 1974; OR
- there is court action pending against you.

If you are applying for a post that is exempt from the provisions of the Act, (normally those dealing directly with children and vulnerable adults), you must disclose ALL criminal convictions found against you. The letter enclosed with the application form will confirm if the post is exempt and therefore what you must declare.

Declaration

- Please provide the name and job title of any relative, friend or acquaintance employed by Cambridgeshire County Council. If you fail to disclose any relationship, which is known to you, you will be disqualified from appointment or, if appointed, may be dismissed without notice.
- The canvassing of a Councillor or Council employee will also disqualify you from appointment.
- Please ensure that you read this statement and that you sign and date the application form.

Monitoring Form

The County Council will complete the 'Reference No'. Please complete the rest of this form, which will be removed from your application form as soon as we receive it and used for monitoring purposes only.

E-mail may be used to contact you, but the address will not be passed onto the recruiting manager.

Code of Conduct

The Council's Code of Conduct details the standards of behaviour that the County Council expects from its employees and people applying for posts within the Council. The County Council, therefore, expects that applicants will:

- tell the truth on their application form and at any interview;
- disclose criminal convictions as appropriate;
- disclose links or membership of any secret society or organisation whose aims may be thought to conflict with Council policy; and
- disclose friendships or relationships to Councillors/Council employees.

The County Council expects that applicants will not:

- try to get Councillors or Council employees to show them undue favour before or during the selection process; OR
- conceal any fact that they should disclose.

'Always complete and attach any accompanying documents, such as equal opportunities monitoring or health history forms. Failure to do so might eliminate your application straightaway.'

Quote from a recruitment specialist

Do read the forms very carefully and follow any instructions exactly; your application may be rejected out of hand if you don't. And remember, if you are working on a paper version, work on a photocopy of the form until you're happy you've got it exactly right. When you've completed it, keep a copy for reference for when you get invited to interview.

Although the form you receive when you apply for a job may not be exactly the same as this one, it is likely to have much in common. Applicants who are using this form from Cambridgeshire County Council are also given written advice on how to complete the form. If you are offered advice always follow it precisely. You will see that you can complete the form and send it in online. However, if you fill it in by hand you must use black ink (this is so it can be easily photocopied). Whilst most of the sections will be easy for you to complete, you must take special care with the section 'How you meet the selection criteria'.

The advice given along with the form tells you that the essential criteria against which your application will be judged is the person specification, so you would need to study that document carefully. Although they show competencies, you are asked specifically to address the person specification item. These advice guidelines give a series of questions to consider.

'How do your abilities and experience make you suitable for the post?'

Use the STAR method to answer this question.

'Why are you applying for this post?'

The employer does not expect answers such as *'It's on my bus route',* or *'The pay is good'.* They want to hear why you want to work for THEM and what you can offer THEM. So your answers should include something along the lines of *'I am interested in working for your organisation because it has a good reputation for staff development and excellent service'* or *'I am particularly interested in this post because it would allow me to use my existing skills and develop further skills'.* Remember, they look at things mostly from their point of view, not yours.

'If the job requires mobility, can you drive, do you have a clean licence, and do you have use of a car or other motor vehicle?'

Answer this truthfully. If you have a disability and employ a driver/helper, you may like to state that here. It is your choice.

'What are your interests outside work?'

See Chapter two for advice on how to complete this section. Remember to relate your interests to the job whenever possible.

'The biggest mistake we see on application forms is that applicants do not give examples of the skills they are trying to demonstrate in their application. Just stating they have these skills does not provide evidence of their likely competency. However, detailed examples of real work situations give a much clearer indication that the applicant is likely to possess the relevant skills, and therefore more likely to perform successfully in the role.'

Jim Machon, manager of the recruitment team, Cambridgeshire County Council

---

Another possible section

One large employer asks on their application form for your experience of working in a group. Ideally, they want a work group, but they say they will accept school/college experience. Some examples of group work and what they are trying to achieve would be as follows.

Group achievement examples

Group	Achievement
Group project work at school, university or work	*'Completed project on local history, meeting deadline. Our group achieved a grade A.'*
Fund-raising activities	*'Raised £1,250 with fun run for SCOPE.'*
Working as part of a team	*'We worked well together for the local history project, each taking a separate section but meeting regularly and helping each other as necessary.'*
Planning a party with others	*'I was on the class committee, which arranged a very successful end-of-year party.'*
Member of football club committee	*'We ensure that health and safety regulations are always adhered to.'*

If you are then asked what you enjoyed about working with other people in the group, be honest – there will be things you enjoyed. Common answers might include:

- learning from each other
- helping each other to be creative
- working towards a goal
- socialising.

If you are asked what you did not enjoy about working with a group, again, be honest. Groups are great, they can achieve so much more than individuals working alone. But they can also be frustrating. Common problems you may have noticed are:

- some people saying too much
- others saying too little
- some people doing a lot of work
- others doing very little
- some people being late and/or unreliable
- people having impractical ideas
- people getting off the point.

And what did you learn about yourself and how you work with other people? Did you learn that you were:

- creative
- patient
- impatient
- hard-working
- always late
- a natural leader
- good at fine detail
- good at cheering people up
- good at finding out information
- happiest sticking to the rules

- thoughtful towards others
- jokey
- challenging
- argumentative.

These are all things a prospective employer would be interested to know. Select carefully those items to include, remember to consider what is needed in the job. By the way, if you realise that you have some negative points here – perhaps you are impatient or always late, do work to rectify this. Problems such as this will hold you back in your career.

'Always retain a copy of your application form. If you get an interview, it will remind you of what you said.'

Quote from a careers adviser

Applying for Apprenticeships

If you want to apply for a government-funded Apprenticeship or Advanced Apprenticeship for young people in England, or a similar programme elsewhere, you should contact your Connexions service for information on opportunities in your area. Apprenticeships are available in around 80 broad areas of work! They allow you to work, earn money and gain nationally-recognised qualifications.

It is possible to make an application through:

- an employer
- an appropriate learning provider – these are organisations that manage Apprenticeships, they are usually further education colleges or private training providers.

You can start the ball rolling by phoning the national Apprenticeships helpline (Tel: 08000 150 600), which can help you to find local learning providers and employers, or visit the website at www.apprenticeships.org.uk

Many young people apply for training during their final year at school, with a view to starting in the summer months, especially if the training is linked to a college course that begins on a particular date. However, you can start most programmes at any time. Be aware that some

Apprenticeships have closing dates very early in the year.

After applying, you can expect to attend interviews, and in some cases you will also be given assessment tests.

Each organisation offering Apprenticeships has its own application form. Whilst they vary, each asks for similar information. In addition to the factual information about your name, address and so on, they may ask questions such as, 'Why do you want this type of Apprenticeship?' This is your chance to present yourself effectively by using the same principles of researching yourself, the work area and the programme. For that reason, if you have not read the whole of this chapter yet, you should do so before reading further.

Why do you want this Apprenticeship?

Don't write something too simplistic like, *'I want to be a beautician'* or *'I'd like to be a builder'.* This section is your opportunity to show that you have really thought about yourself, the content of the Apprenticeship programme, and the employer or training organisation you are applying to.

Are you clear about what you will have to do to complete the Apprenticeship? Most involve some study at college, possibly on day- or block-release from work. You will take a relevant NVQ based on your performance at work, a technical certificate to demonstrate your knowledge in the area (e.g. a BTEC or OCR qualification) and key skills.

Below are some questions you could ask yourself – use the answers in your application.

- What interests you about this type of work?

- Do you have any previous experience in this area of work, for instance through school work experience, part-time jobs, voluntary work or helping family members?

- Do any courses you have taken already relate to the Apprenticeship you want to do? For example, you may have taken a GCSE in applied business, which would be helpful for an Apprenticeship in business administration.

- Have you talked to someone who works in your chosen field? This would demonstrate that you have done some research and know what is involved.

- What are your future career plans?

Here is an example of what one person wrote on her Apprenticeship application.

'I am interested in an Advanced Apprenticeship in children's care, learning and development, as I would like to work in a nursery. I have considerable experience of working with children – I have two younger brothers who I look after a lot, and I regularly babysit for neighbours' children. In addition, I have had two weeks of work experience at Happy Days Nursery. Mrs Jones at the nursery has provided me with a reference.

I enjoy working with children and relate to them well. I am patient and caring with a lot of energy. I believe that I have a good understanding of the needs of children and enjoy helping them to develop. I like working alongside other nursery staff as part of a team, particularly on projects such as theme weeks. Following advice from Mrs Jones, I have found I am quite confident when speaking to parents about the needs of their children.

Last year I completed seven GCSEs, which are listed. As you will see, one of these was home economics: child development, for which I got an A.

The Apprenticeship will give me the opportunity to gain real work experience and to achieve recognised qualifications at the same time.'

With a little research, thinking about what you have to offer and the Apprenticeship on offer, you can complete a successful Apprenticeship application form.

'I love the mistakes some people make. One person wrote, 'I am a rabid shorthand typist.' She obviously wasn't a rabid spell checker!'

Quote from a manager of a training company

Chapter checklist

When completing your application form, have you:

- taken at least one photocopy before you start? – remember to work on that copy until you are sure you have it exactly right

- read the instructions on the form carefully and followed them to the letter?

- read the job description, person specification and any information you have about the company thoroughly?

- tried to work out exactly what type of person the organisation is looking for by studying their selection criteria?

- analysed your skills, experience and personality, highlighting those things that fit in with the needs of the job you're applying for?

- presented information about yourself on the 'supporting information' section of the application form in the same order as in the selection criteria?

- been consistent with the way you present material? – make it easy for the reader to shortlist you!

- left the form after the first draft, so that you have an opportunity to rethink what you've written?

- polished the form until you are completely happy that it gets across exactly the message you want?

- made a good copy with no mistakes?

- kept a copy for future reference?

- remembered your covering letter?

Chapter eight

University and college applications

You should read this chapter:

- if you are going to apply for a higher education course through UCAS, or

- you are going to apply for a course at a college of further education.

By the end of this chapter you should know:

- how to go about completing the factual sections of your application form

- how to present yourself positively in your personal statement, or 'other information' section.

UCAS applications

Applications for most full-time undergraduate courses – leading to Diplomas of Higher Education, foundation degrees, Higher National qualifications and first degrees – at universities and colleges of higher education are through UCAS. (A few courses may still require direct application to the institution concerned.)

You will make your UCAS application through Apply – a secure, web-based application system which, with a buzzword from your school, college or Connexions service, you can use anywhere with internet access. To use Apply you need to register online on the UCAS website – www.ucas.com

Most of the information you will need is in the booklet *Your Online Application* – this can be downloaded from the UCAS website. Read this through carefully before you begin – it will save you time, effort and frustration. Check that you have the most up-to-date information, for instance, there are certain dates by which your application should reach UCAS.

Once you begin completing the factual information in the application, help text will appear to guide you through each section. This process should be straightforward. It is the personal statement section where you have the opportunity to come alive as a person. These days, not many applicants are invited to interview. Most are selected purely on their application and exam results. This means that you have to convince admissions tutors on paper that you are the right person for the course!

Your personal statement

This is probably the most important part of your application, because it is this, along with the statement from your referee, on which selectors rely heavily when making a decision about whether or not to offer you a place. Apply allows you to write up to 4,000 characters (including spaces), so you have to be clear and concise. UCAS recommends that you prepare your personal statement using a wordprocessing package and then copy and paste it into your application in Apply.

It's a good idea to use headings and paragraphs to structure your personal statement. It's up to you what you include, but you could cover all or some of the following:

- why you have chosen the courses you have listed – what particularly interests you about the subject(s) – including details of what you have read

- your future plans or career aspirations

- any work experience, placement, job or voluntary work you have done, particularly if it is relevant to your subject choice

- any subjects you are studying that do not have a formal assessment

- details of skills and achievements you have gained through activities such as Young Enterprise, the Duke of Edinburgh's Award or Millennium Volunteers

- any sponsorship or placements you have or have applied for

- your social, sport or leisure interests – any positions of responsibility held, etc

- your reasons for deferring your entry if you are planning a gap year

- any involvement in schemes for widening participation, such as summer schools or master classes.

You may want to include information from your national record of achievement or Progress File, if you have one.

Here's what one admissions tutor for a teaching course had to say about some of the applications she has seen ...

'When I read through the applications prior to interview I look for a real commitment to wanting to teach. Candidates must show that they have done some work with youngsters. I don't want to think that they have just decided 'Oh, it might be a good idea to work with children'. I need to see a real commitment to the work. I like to be convinced, even on paper, that there is a sense of real warmth towards children. That can come across even on the application because of the way they describe the work they have done with children in the past.

Sadly, some prospective students come across as very naive and not very politically (with a small p) aware. That is, they don't seem to know what's going on in the teaching world, they don't seem to have read the Times Educational Supplement, or to be aware of current issues in education. We would like to see this type of awareness on the application, because we want to know that students know that the job is a difficult one and that finding employment at the end of the course is not always easy.

When I read through the applications they are sometimes so poor that I suspect that the applicants haven't shown them to anyone else before they send them off. I suppose it could feel a bit embarrassing for some people to do so, but it would be of real help to get an objective view before they apply. After all, they must know that people are going to read them. If they did get someone else to check them, they wouldn't make such basic mistakes. They really need to find someone they can trust to go through their application with them and to question them on it.

For example, during the interview I will often take a phrase from the applicant's personal statement and start my question by saying, 'You say in your application ...' This means that if they haven't thought through a statement they've made they can be left with egg on their face at interview. When completing an application, students should always have the interview in mind as well.

Sometimes after I've actually interviewed the person I feel a need to go back to re-read their application to see if what they wrote ties up with what they were saying.

> *One big question I always keep in mind – would I want this person to teach my child for a year?'*

Many people really hate completing the dreaded blank page ('Other/ further information' section) of an application form, but you could try to think of it as doing a piece of work; an essay on the world's most interesting person – you. Suddenly it seems much more appealing. What do you do with any essay? You:

- read the question and attempt to fully understand what is expected of you

- read all the relevant material to formulate an answer

- select those aspects of the material needed for your essay, rejecting those that are inappropriate
- plan how to present your information, considering all aspects, angles and arguments
- write an essay plan
- do a draft
- refine it as many times as it takes to get it right
- make a good copy.

And that's exactly what you have to do with your personal statement. Don't expect to finish it in one sitting. Start the work and then leave it for a while, mulling it over in your mind as you go about the rest of your life. Once you have decided what to say, polish and polish it until it gleams! It should take you several goes. Remember to get one or two other people to read it before you send it off, preferably a teacher.

The chapters on CV writing in this book give you a list of positive words you can use to describe yourself and your achievements; you might want to refer back to them when you get started.

If you have been working through this book you will already have in your notebook details of your skills, experience, education, character, interests, leisure activities, strengths and weaknesses, special awards, etc. These will help you, but don't include any weaknesses!

Remembering what the admissions tutor had to say earlier in this section, do keep in mind current issues in the area of your choice. You can get information from:

- the internet
- newspapers
- professional or trade journals (your reference library will probably have them)
- talking to people already doing the job your course could lead to
- speaking to existing students.

Activity

Here is an example of what someone might write in their personal statement. Work through the paragraphs asking yourself what you like and what you would change. (Each paragraph is numbered for later reference.)

1. *'I am applying for the business HND course because I am interested in business and I want a good career.'*

2. *'I have become interested in business because a family friend works in a bank and I realise that I must get a good qualification to start my career in a junior management position.'*

3. *'I worked in a building society for three weeks for work experience. I know that this isn't quite the same as a bank but I learned a lot of useful things.'*

4. *'I am currently taking seven GCSEs including business studies, which I enjoy very much. I particularly like learning about the way the financial world works.'*

5. *'My ambition is to be a bank manager or to work for a large finance company.'*

6. *'I enjoy playing netball and going to the cinema. I also enjoy embroidery and am a keen photographer.'*

7. *'I have just passed my First Aid Certificate with the British Red Cross.'*

8. *'I have not yet secured an industrial placement, but have applied to three banks and am awaiting their response.'*

Do not read any further until you have completed this exercise.

General points

The first thing to note is that nearly every paragraph started with 'I' (not uncommonly seen). Try to make your beginnings more varied. Further, the whole thing is a bit disjointed with no 'flow' to the content. Although it provides quite a lot of relevant information, it is stilted and uninspiring. Many of the points should be expanded in more detail.

There's probably a lot of information to cover in your personal statement; do check that you have included everything necessary and that you have done so in a logical order. This will make it easier for the reader to shortlist you for the course.

Specific points

Here are some suggestions as to how each paragraph could be improved. You may have thought of others.

1. *'I am applying for the business HND course because I am interested in business and I want a good career.'*

This is clearly far too brief an answer. The applicant should have mentioned particular aspects of the course that are appealing. It's good to provide information on career aspirations, but this is too general.

2. *'I have become interested in business because a family friend works in a bank and I realise that I must get a good qualification to start my career in a junior management position.'*

It can be helpful to state that you know someone working in a particular field because it shows that you are likely to have a deeper than average knowledge of the work, and that you are likely to get support from them. It also means that you are likely to have realistic expectations about the career area. However, the two halves of the sentence don't really 'hang together'. There are better ways to word the whole lot, but at the very least there should be a full stop after the word 'bank'. Perhaps the first half could read, *'I feel that I have a good understanding of business from a banking perspective as a family friend works in a bank. This means that I am very familiar with the type of work involved.'* It may even be helpful here to give examples of the work, and in a completely rewritten version, these examples could be linked to the work experience.

The second half of the sentence would probably be better elsewhere – perhaps when explaining the reasons for applying for the course.

3. *'I worked in a building society for three weeks for work experience. I know that this isn't quite the same as a bank but I learned a lot of useful things.'*

Ouch! What a lot of missed opportunities here. For a start, never put yourself or your skills down (*'I know it isn't quite the same ...'* – the reader knows that too, there's no need to emphasise it). Here are some pointers about this section:

- it doesn't give any feeling of enthusiasm – the applicant is saying they want to work in this type of environment, but gives no indication of having enjoyed it

- there is much overlap between working in a building society and working in a bank, especially as building societies offer many banking facilities; the applicant would have learned many transferable skills that could have been mentioned – dealing with people, handling money, filing, understanding systems, answering the telephone, liaising with other branches and using a computer, to name but a few

- the applicant could have mentioned the aspects of the work that he or she particularly enjoyed and those that he or she is keen to learn more about (ensuring, obviously, that the course being applied for covers these aspects). This would have demonstrated that the applicant was familiar with the course content.

4. *'I am currently taking seven GCSEs including business studies, which I enjoy very much. I particularly like learning about the way the financial world works.'*

This is better inasmuch as it shows some enthusiasm. However, the applicant could have expanded further on the aspect of the business studies course that he or she enjoyed. It would also be worth noting any other related topics to business studies – an obvious example would be maths if the person is thinking about going into banking. Another example would be any course that involves analytical thinking, as business studies would certainly require this. Again, this would be a transferable skill. Another useful thing to do would be to highlight how any aspects of her/his studies had proved valuable in work experience.

5. *'My ambition is to be a bank manager or to work for a large finance company.'*

It's a good idea to state career aspirations, but don't repeat information provided elsewhere.

6. *'I enjoy playing netball and going to the cinema. I also enjoy embroidery and am a keen photographer.'*

This is a good start, and the fact that the applicant makes time to pursue leisure interests as well as study will be seen positively by the reader. Also, it shows that the applicant has some social and some solitary interests that are quite varied – this shows a 'rounded person'.

However, it could be much improved:

- the word 'enjoy' is used twice in two sentences – use instead another similar word

- it might interest the reader to know who the applicant plays netball for – is it for the school, a local team or a national team? Does the applicant have any special responsibilities as part of the team, perhaps organising return matches or refreshments?

- netball is a team game – a business course is sure to involve some team working, probably on a business project with other students; it would, therefore, be worth him or her mentioning that they enjoy being part of a team

- although it's unlikely that the cinema going will link directly with the course, if the applicant enjoys one particular type of film it could just be mentioned ('especially thrillers') – this is unlikely to help them get on a course, but it might give the admissions tutor something to talk about if he or she is called for an interview, especially if they enjoy the same films – it never hurts to have something in common!

- embroidery shows attention to detail, a skill needed in business – a connection could be made here

- what sort of photography – general, still life, birds, people or sunsets? Like the cinema visits, it may pay the applicant to expand just a little on this section.

7. *'I have just passed my First Aid Certificate with the British Red Cross.'*

The reader might wonder why this person chose to do this certificate. It may be that there is a reason, such as helping in a Brownie pack, which they have omitted to mention (you need a lot of leadership skills to run any sort of group).

8. *'I have not yet secured an industrial placement, but have applied to three banks and am awaiting their response.'*

This is fine, although perhaps a little more detail would help. Which banks? Is the applicant hopeful of the outcome?

There you have it, one personal statement analysed. Now it's your turn!

Sample personal statement

The following is an example of how to structure your personal statement – yours can be quite a bit longer than this ... don't forget you are allowed up to 4,000 characters.

'I am applying for the degree in social work because this is a career I feel very enthusiastic about.

At present I am studying for A levels in psychology, English and sociology. I am particularly enjoying psychology because of the understanding it has given me into why people behave as they do. Whilst psychology provides this knowledge from an individual perspective, sociology looks at what makes people tick from the other end of the spectrum – society. Additionally, I have studied for a Diploma of Achievement course on probability and risk, as I believe that much social work involves assessing risk.

In year 9, I undertook a two-week work placement in a residential home for elderly people and very much enjoyed working with both the staff and residents. I came into contact regularly with other people in various caring professions and have a good grasp of the concept of partnership working. This, plus conversations with my mother (a social worker) and her colleagues, has given me a good insight into the issues faced by social workers.

I am a pupil mentor for our school and am currently mentoring two year 7 students. Our training for this role was very relevant and covered understanding people, and listening and questioning skills.

My interests are socialising with friends, being a member of an amateur dramatics group and reading 'family' novels. I have learned the value of teamwork through the dramatics group, and can also use my initiative readily.'

Applications for further education

Unlike applications to higher education, there is no centralised system for applying for further education courses. Further education includes courses up to level 3 – that's up to AS/A level standard. You may want to do a course leading to a BTEC, OCR or City & Guilds qualification, or to an NVQ, for instance.

Most people apply to a college near their home. For courses in certain subjects, such as agriculture, you may need to apply further afield to a more specialist college.

Further education colleges produce full-time course prospectuses and have websites with all sorts of information about the college and the courses on offer.

Once you have decided which course you want to do and where, you will need to complete an application form. This may be a separate form, a pull-out sheet in the prospectus, or you may be able to apply online.

Start by reading the form carefully. You may be asked to use black ink and/or to write in capitals. Fill in all the factual details as accurately as possible. You will be asked for your name, contact details, qualifications and other relevant information. Speak to someone at the college if you are unsure how to answer any of the questions. There is usually someone in student services who can help.

You may be asked to briefly state your reasons for applying for the course of your choice. You could mention:

- what interests you about the subject

- any relevant work experience

- why you have chosen the particular college – it might have excellent facilities for your subject, have a good reputation for the course you want to do, etc.

Once you have completed your form on paper or online, make sure that you send it in good time – some courses fill up very quickly. If you are called for an interview, re-read your form in case you are asked questions about what you have written.

'What students have to remember is that we read literally dozens of applications each year. I certainly love to see one that stands out from the crowd in some way. I think, 'Oh good, this'll be an interesting interview.'

Quote from a college lecturer

Chapter checklist

Have you:

- read the form and/or instructions for application carefully?

- presented factual information in a clear and consistent way?

- followed the instructions exactly?

- included all the relevant information about your reasons for applying for the course(s) of your choice?

Chapter nine

Covering letters

You should read this chapter:

- when you have completed your CV or application form.

By the end of this chapter you should know:

- what points to consider when writing a covering letter
- who to address the letter to
- how to write letters when applying for a specific job or speculatively.

The importance of covering letters

Your covering letter can be as important as your CV or application form, yet they are often poorly written or overlooked altogether. The covering letter is usually the first thing a shortlister sees, so you must make the most of this opportunity to further sell yourself as a person, as well as to highlight any major points you think will impress. It is a quick introduction to you and your skill set, and, as such, saves the shortlister time and effort.

Making a start

If you are sending a CV, you may have chosen to leave out some of the 'additional information' at the end of your CV to form the meat of your covering letter. If you've completed an application form, the odds are that the layout of the form didn't give you much opportunity to say everything you wanted to say.

But let's do the easy bit first. Whether you are writing in response to a particular job advert, or speculatively, you must get the letter to the correct person. This may be obvious if the name was stated in the advertisement or was with the information sent to you by the organisation. However, if it wasn't or if you are writing speculatively, spend the time and effort to find out who the correct person is. It's a small but important point, because it shows the reader that you are able to use your initiative. You simply have to phone the organisation and ask the switchboard who would be the correct person.

Be prepared though. Often switchboard operators don't listen well and before you know where you are they've put you through to the personnel manager (or whoever) without having given you their name or you asking them to do so. So instead of a nice informal chat to the operator, you're speaking instantly to the decision maker. If that leaves you saying 'Um, um' a few times, you won't make a good impression. So prepare beforehand what you want to say if this happens. If you are inexperienced at speaking to people 'in authority' make a few notes of what you want to say and have these in front of you. These include what job you are interested in – also noting where you found out about the job and any job reference number, some basic facts about yourself that relate to the job and why you are interested in the job.

'I advertised for editors for our publishing firm. I couldn't believe it when several people sent me scruffy covering letters. A couple were written on lined A4 paper torn from a pad. They went straight in the bin along with their CVs.'

Quote from a director of a publishing company

Practical issues

Your covering letter should be on good-quality A4 writing paper, preferably the same as your CV if you've sent one, or on unlined writing paper. DON'T use lined A4 paper with holes punched down the side, the pretty paper Aunt Mary sent you last Christmas, or anything else. IT WON'T IMPRESS and you'll simply look unprofessional.

Layout for letters is usually aligned left, that means:

- no indents

- everything lined up to the left but 'ragged' on the right.

Also:

- punctuation marks are not used after the address

- the date is written in full but without 'th', 'rd', etc – for example 3 July 2007

- the main heading is highlighted in some way, usually with bold type. If you are handwriting the letter (and some employers ask you to do this), the heading can be written in capitals or underlined.

- use 'Yours sincerely' if you write to the person by name – if you really can't find out the person's name and have to write anonymously, it's 'Dear Sir or Madam', and 'Yours faithfully' – note that 'sincerely' and 'faithfully' do not start with capital letters

- write 'Enc.' at the bottom of your letter to show that you have enclosed something (your CV, application form or anything else)

- remember to include your telephone number and email address in the letter somewhere, either under your address or in the body of the letter – I know this information will be on the CV or application form, but make it easy for them to phone you.

Here is what I mean:

> **Your address**
> etc
> etc
> etc
> **postcode**
>
> **telephone and mobile numbers**
> **email address**
>
>
> Bloggs Engineering Works
> Unit 7
> St Martins Industrial Estate
> Bloxburg
> Avon BB22 3EE
>
> Date
>
> Dear Ms Stedman
>
> **Vacancy for Trainee Engineer**
>
> Opening comments.
>
>
> Body of your letter, may take one or more paragraphs.
>
>
> Final sentence.
>
>
> Yours sincerely
>
> Your name (printed clearly under your signature)
>
> Enc.

Occasionally you will be asked to write the covering letter by hand. Generally this means that they want to check your handwriting because they want to ensure that it is legible, because this is necessary for the job. Just occasionally they plan to get a graphologist to analyse it to make an assessment of your personality. Graphology isn't used terribly widely, so it's more likely to be the first reason. Obviously, this means that you need to use your 'best' handwriting.

Whether your letter is handwritten, typed or wordprocessed make sure that you write using good grammer and spellin (better than this, that is ...). If you are unsure, ask someone you trust to check it.

'In your covering letter, explain why you are interested in this type of work, demonstrating an understanding of what it is likely to involve.'

Quote from a recruitment specialist

Content

Your covering letter should sound confident and lively. It should tell the reader in very brief terms (using bullet points or not – the choice is yours) why you'd be good for the job. Don't overdo it and look pushy or big-headed, but simply let them know what you can do. This means that you have to summarise in no more than about four or five sentences what you've said in the CV or application form. You may choose to add some new information, perhaps the fact that you'd like to move to that area, or when you are available for interview. Remember to use all those positive sounding words again. Remember too, to use some of the words in any information you have received about the job.

A good general format is shown below.

- Paragraph 1 – a brief introduction to yourself including a description of the job you are applying for, or your 'career objective'. Give details of why you want this particular job with this particular organisation. Sound enthusiastic. Show you've done your research.

- Paragraphs 2/3 – a short description of your education, skills, competencies and any other information you think they should know. Remember to target everything you write to the vacancy you are applying for.

- Paragraph 4 – positive final comments, then give your availability for interview, or say that you would like an opportunity to visit them if your letter is being written speculatively.

Remember also to use key words to attract the attention of the person or software package reading your letter. If necessary, mention any negative points in your application if you can explain them away.

On the next few pages are some advertisements and the covering letters to go with each.

Advertisement

Direct Marketing Assistant

Griffin Ltd are looking for a well motivated and enthusiastic person to join their small marketing department. The person appointed will be part of a team responsible for the direct marketing promotion of the company.

We are looking for someone with an interest in learning how to:

- copywrite and proofread
- analyse campaign data
- liaise with other departments and printers.

You should be a good communicator both verbally and in writing. Keyboard skills are an advantage.

Please send your CV and covering letter to (contact details).

'When writing your covering letter remember to weave in some of the words from the selection criteria.'

Quote from a CV writing expert

Covering letter

John Farnsworth
Griffin Ltd
27 Dallow Road
York YO1 2XX

1 December 2007

Dear Mr Farnsworth

Direct Marketing Assistant

I am very interested in the direct marketing assistant post advertised in this week's *Recorder* and enclose my CV for your consideration.

I have recently left Colmsford Regional College where I successfully[1] completed a BTEC in business studies. I particularly enjoyed the module on marketing[2] and went on to do a six-week placement with Briggs Hardware in their marketing department[3].

While at Briggs, I learned to use wordprocessing and desktop publishing packages[4]. Last year I was deputy editor of the student magazine and these skills were fully tested there.

I would love[5] to work in direct marketing, especially at Griffins as I feel it is an exciting field at the moment[6].

Yours sincerely,

Well, as an employer I'd be reaching for the phone to see this person ...

1. Two selling points in one sentence. S/he has 'successfully' completed the course (positive word) and mentioned a very relevant course, too.

2. Likewise, 'enjoyed' and mentioned the most relevant module.

3. This placement must have offered a lot of valuable skills, pity they weren't mentioned in a little more detail.

4. This is a higher level of computer literacy than many college leavers attain, and is certainly worth highlighting.

5. Is this a bit gushing? Perhaps, but it comes across and sincere and enthusiastic, but remember to say why Griffins and not another similar firm.

6. Why is it an exciting field 'at the moment'? If the writer knows, it demonstrates up-to-date knowledge, and to finish the sentence by briefly saying why would be a bonus.

TRAINEE WINDSCREEN FITTER

Screensafe plc is looking for a trainee to join their team of windscreen fitters. Body shop experience would be an advantage.

Please apply to:

Screensafe plc
Screensafe House
66–71 High Street
Northton NO1 2SS

Dear Mr Proto[1]

[2]

I am writing to apply for your job as a Trainee Windscreen Fitter[3]. I think I would enjoy this sort of work as I spend a lot of time helping family and friends to repair their cars[4]. I also go to car maintenance classes at Coltree Evening Centre[5].

I am enclosing my CV and hope to hear from you soon[6].

Yours sincerely,

> *'I like people to give their email address in their covering letter. It makes it easy for me to invite them to interview.'*

> ### Quote from a manager of a retail store

This letter certainly gives a lot of useful information, but could be improved nevertheless:

1. The writer has bothered to phone Screensafe and find out who to address the letter to. This shows initiative.

2. Always put a heading on your letter. It makes it easier to read and refer back to. If the organisation is advertising several vacancies it makes it easier for them to keep track of which letters belong where.

3. Tell the employer where you saw the advertisement.

4. This sentence is both good and bad. It comes across as enthusiastic and that's always good, but it also seems rather as if you're telling the employer what they can do for you rather than what you can do for them. Perhaps it could be reworded along the lines of, *'I have experience of stripping engines and replacing spare parts. I have helped respray an old Mini. I very much enjoy this type of work and go to car ...'*

5. Good to mention going to evening class, it shows real commitment.

6. Why not make this last sentence more sparky? *'I am enclosing my CV and hope you will feel that I have the qualities to make a good windscreen fitter.'*

HIGH MEADOWS HOUSING

Customer Services Clerk

We are looking for a lively and enthusiastic person to fill this very important post. The job involves taking customer details, quoting prices and inputting data onto computer. The ability to deal tactfully with other companies and departments, as well as with customers, is vital.

Previous experience of this type of work would be an advantage.

Contact:
Mrs Mari Singh
Customer Services Manager
High Meadows Housing
High Meadows
Clydesfield CL3 2DH

Dear Mrs Singh

Re: Customer Services Clerk

Your advertisement in this week's Recorder interests me very much. I am currently working as an Administrative Assistant for Briggs Ltd and feel that I have very relevant skills[1] for this vacancy. I am:

- experienced at dealing with customers
- familiar with Word and Excel
- experienced at liaising with other departments[2].

I am enclosing my CV and hope that you will give me an interview[3].

Yours sincerely

'I am always impressed when candidates put something in the covering letter that shows they are aware of what's going on in our company or industry. It shows initiative and makes me more willing to shortlist them.'

Quote from a manager in an IT company

This is one way to lay out a covering letter – using bullet points again to highlight your skills. Here are some points you may have noticed about this letter.

1. This is a confident sentence, which should keep the reader reading.

2. Good list of skills. The writer hasn't pointed out that s/he has no experience of giving quotes, it's simply implied by omission. That's fine because the advertisement only says 'previous experience would be an advantage' so they'll be willing to give someone training if necessary.

3. Although the list of skills is good, there is no mention of personal qualities. From the advertisement I am sure the postholder would need tact, good attention to detail, ability to keep calm under stress, good communication skills. The writer could have mentioned these even if they are already in the CV. Remember, if the employer gets a huge response they may not bother to read the CV if the covering letter is poor.

SCHUMACHER LTD

is looking for a

MACHINE/SETTER OPERATOR

to work as part of a team in our busy production department. You will need the ability to use simple tools to ensure that all our machinery is kept in good running order. Full training will be given, although you must be capable of working on your own initiative once trained. The job involves heavy lifting. You must be literate and numerate and able to pass an aptitude text. Hours 6am–3pm or 3pm–10pm.

Contact:
The Personnel Department
Schumacher Ltd
Smyth Industrial Estate
Colmsworth CO8 4MT

Dear Mr McGregor[1]

[2]

I am writting[3] about your job[4] in the Recorder for a Machine Setter/Operator.

Please find enclosed my CV. I am leaving school next month and think I would be good at this sort of work[5].

I hope you will consider me for an interview[6].

Yours faithfully[7]

Oops! I doubt if this person would get an interview if there was much other choice.

1. This shows initiative, because the advertisement didn't show the name of the person to contact, and the applicant has bothered to find out.

2. No heading!

3. Not good enough. The advertisement states that they're looking for someone who is literate. This person should have got someone to check the spelling before sending the letter off.

4. This sentence is poorly worded. It was an *a job vacancy* for a machine/setter operator, not a *job*.

5. Mmm, so the person thinks they'd be good for the job, but has failed to try to convince the reader of the fact. S/he should have said why.

6. This sounds a bit grovelling. The sentence could be reworded to sound more positive. Perhaps something like '*I am sure you will agree that I have potential for this type of work and hope you will grant me an interview.*'

7. Because the letter starts '*Dear Mr McGregor*', it should end with '*Yours sincerely*', not '*Yours faithfully*'.

Activity

Look at the advertisement below. What comments can you make about the covering letter?

TRAINEE RECRUITMENT CONSULTANT

First Time Recruitment

Central Birmingham

You will be an ambitious graduate, resilient and looking for an exciting and challenging career. Ideally with some sales experience, a knowledge of the Care Sector would be advantage but is not essential.

Contact:
Gemma Middleton
Branch Manager
First Time Recruitment
52 Kimberley Road
Birmingham BM23 4RR

---

7 August 2008

Dear Ms Middleton

Trainee Recruitment Consultant

Your advertisement in this week's *Birmingham Gazette* was of great interest to me, because I am a recent graduate with the experience you seek.

Whilst studying for my English honours degree at ARU University, Cambridge, where I obtained a 2.1, I undertook three vacation jobs, all of which are relevant to your vacancy. The first was as an administrator in our local Social Services office. This gave me an excellent overview of the care field. The second was working for Pegasus Recruitment in Nuneaton, where I took, logged in and interviewed prospective candidates. The third was selling advertising space for the *Birmingham Gazette*. I believe this combination of experience means I am very well suited to your work. Additionally, I am a hardworking, reliable person with good communication skills.

You will find my CV attached and I hope, once you have read it, that you will be able to offer me an interview.

Yours sincerely,

Covering letters for 'on spec' CVs

Sometimes you may decide to write to an employer speculatively, known as 'on spec' – where no job is advertised, but you think you will write anyway and try your luck. This can be a very worthwhile approach. Chapter one gives some information on when to write these letters, and there is an example of a speculative letter on page 170.

Sample covering letters

10 Gilbert Avenue
Anytown
Glos GL2 3BL
01222 343536

Mr J. Brown
Corfield Industries
Unit 4, Anytown Industrial Estate
Anytown
Glos GL5 5PL

3 May 2007

Dear Mr Brown

Career Goal: Clerical vacancy

I read in yesterday's *Anytown Gazette* that Corfield Industries is extending its operations in the near future and taking on additional staff. I am writing to ask if you would consider me for one of your clerical vacancies. I leave Anytown Regional College in June, by which time I will have taken my BTEC in business studies.

I have enjoyed the business studies course very much, particularly the sections on finance and administration. My coursework grades have always been very good.

I have already put my learning to good use in my work placement with Jones Pharmaceuticals Ltd, where I shadowed their Accounts Clerk. Through her excellent instruction I quickly learned how to use Excel (and have followed up this learning in my own time). Within a week I was making entries, dealing with simple enquiries and generally finding my way around.

An energetic person, I feel I can offer Corfield's not only my experience but my enthuasiasm, motivation and willingness to learn.

I will contact you within the next few days and hope to speak to you further then.

Yours sincerely

229 Main Street
Shireton
Cambs SH4 4EE
01225 763421

Mrs Amez
Manager
Wonder Pizza Co
23 High Street
Shireton SH7 7OO

4 April 2008

Dear Mrs Amez

Seeking: Vacancy for Chef

Your advertisement in today's *Shireton Evening News* interested me very much because this is just the type of work I am looking for, and I believe I have a lot of relevant experience to offer your company.

I am enclosing my CV for your information, and from it you will see that I have one year's experience as a waitress and one year working in the kitchen for Giovanni's Restaurant whilst completing my education and City and Guilds Catering. Giovanni's would, I feel sure, be very happy to provide a reference for me.

In addition to my qualifications and experience I can also offer you my:

- enthusiasm
- ability to learn quickly
- willingness to continue training
- customer service skills
- ability to work in a busy kitchen
- knowledge of hygiene.

I hope that you will be interested in my application and that I will have an opportunity to discuss this further with you at interview.

Yours sincerely

19 King's Street
Redfearn
Lanarkshire RD3 3EE
01987 778865

Ms Reed
Personnel Manager
Grigg's Ltd
28 Dalton Street
Darmington DA3 4TT

12 January 2008

Dear Ms Reed

Van Driver Vacancy

Please find attached my application form for the above vacancy, which I saw advertised in today's *Redfearn Weekly*.

As you will see, I have 18 months' experience working for Jones Industries in Redfearn who would, I feel sure, be willing to provide a reference for me. During that time I made deliveries both locally and within a 100-mile radius. I also:

- had an unbroken attendance record
- was always punctual
- was accident free
- had a good reputation with both Jones' staff and customers.

I plan to move to the Darmington area within the next few weeks and am committed to living there. I am available for interview any day after the 27 January and hope to have an opportunity to speak to you then.

Yours sincerely

27 The High Street
Histon
Berkshire HI23 5RT

Beneficial Books plc
20 The Hythe
Colchester CO1 1PP

30 November 2007

Dear Ms Chandler

Finance Clerk – *Colchester Weekly News* **28 January – Ref 27–090**

Your advertisement in the *Colchester Weekly News* was of particular interest to me as I have just finished a two-year business studies course and took an additional unit in finance.

During the course I undertook a work placement with Jones' engineering in their finance department. This was so successful that for the past year, in addition to my college course, I have worked for Jones' for ten hours per week.

My experience and education have given me an excellent grounding in the type of position you are advertising. My energy, commitment and integrity also make me a hardworking and reliable worker.

I would welcome an opportunity to discuss this appointment with you.

Yours sincerely,

'Many companies like to keep CVs sent on spec. When a vacancy comes up it saves them having to advertise. With even a small advert in a local paper costing around £750, this is a big saving.'

Quote from a careers teacher

801 Long Road
Templeton
Devon TM34 5TU

Purley Pizza Parlour
234 Main Road
Purley
PL1 3RF

4 February 2008

Dear Ms Perkins

Work goal: Part-time work

I am a final-year student at Purley Community College and am currently seeking part-time work in the catering business. I have just applied for a place on the City and Guilds culinary arts course run at Action College and feel that the experience working with a reputable company such as your own would be invaluable.

In return I can offer you:

- a conscientious approach – I always meet deadlines and am very reliable
- good customer service skills – I have worked Saturdays for the past year in Progress Paper Shop
- willingness to learn
- flexibility.

As you can see from my CV, I have also taken three cookery courses at evening classes in my spare time, and am currently attending an evening class in business skills.

I am enclosing my CV and would appreciate being considered should any vacancies arise.

Yours sincerely,

'People sending CVs on spec should remember that the organisation receiving them has to destroy them after six months to comply with data protection laws. It may be necessary therefore to send an updated version.'

Quote from a careers adviser

Chapter checklist

Remember that you should:

- always write a covering letter to introduce your CV or application form – the exception to this is for college applications

- use good-quality A4 paper

- use no more than one side of A4 paper

- make sure your handwriting can be read

- address the letter to the decision-maker

- remember to head the letter with the job title and say where you saw the vacancy

- sign letters addressed to a named person with *'Yours sincerely'*

- sign letters addressed to *'Dear Sir'* or *'Dear Madam'* with *'Yours faithfully'*

- use the letter to highlight your strengths in relation to the post

- use the letter to provide any additional information not included in your CV or application form

- consider using bullet points if you want to get a lot of information across

- sound positive and confident, not grovelling and apologetic

- make sure the letter is articulate, pleasant to read, clean and perfect.

Index